TEACHING INQUIRY-BASED SCIENCE

A GUIDE FOR MIDDLE AND HIGH SCHOOL TEACHERS

Mark D. Walker

CONTENTS

ACKNOWLEDGEMENTS

I would most like to acknowledge my former employer Prof. Kirsten Schlüter from the Department of Chemistry and Biology at the University of Siegen, Germany. She gave me the opportunity to work with her developing and finding out about inquiry-based science. I found this work interesting and enjoyable. This was a surprise to me initially. I had always had a rather negative view of teaching. Teaching, I thought, was easy. All you had to do was stand up and say what you knew. It was only while learning about inquiry-based science that I realized it is much more than this. Teaching is an art. It is easy to know something, but much more difficult to communicate that to someone else in a way they will remember. Teaching is a skilled and specialist ability, which not everyone can do. I would like to thank Prof. Schlüter for letting me find this out.

I wrote much of the text parellel to the work I was doing for her. I would like to thank her for the support and understanding she showed while I was doing so. I hope the readers, learn to appreciate and use inquiry in their own classrooms as I feel this would be the best thanks that she could have.

I would also like to thank Angelika Kremer, Bernd Mosler, Dr. Wolfgang Poltz, and Dr. Martin Gröger from the Department for Chemistry and Biology at the University of Siegen for their ideas and support in our research and work into inquiry-based science teaching.

ABOUT THE AUTHOR

Mark Walker is a teaching and research assistant in Biology didactics of the Biology didactics group, part of the Chemistry and Biology department at the University of Siegen, Germany.

HOW TO USE THIS BOOK

This book is designed for middle or high school science teachers wishing to learn more about using inquiry-based science in their classrooms. The book is intended to be a short and concise introduction to inquiry-based science. It aims to be practical, offering a number of examples of inquiry-based science that you could use in your classrooms. However instead of simply providing examples I have tried to write a book which acts as a guidebook, offering general methods which you can use yourself to develop inquiry-based lessons of your own. You don't just want a list of examples; you want to have the tools that enable you to teach what you want. This book tries to suggest general methods that can be used by a teacher and integrated into lessons of their own design. Only when teachers learn how to organize and manage inquiry-based lessons of their own design, without recourse to the examples provided in a textbook will inquiry really become widespread in our schools.

The book is divided into 4 sections. The first section is the 'theory' section where the basic ideas behind inquiry are covered. Most existing teachers will have come across this material before and may find little of interest here. It is included here simply for completeness. The first chapter explains what inquiry-based science is and provides a simple introduction to inquiry. The chapter about scientific inquiry is recommended to those of you with a non-science background, as this area is often neglected in other books about inquiry. The third chapter provides information about the constructivist theory of learning. These first few chapters provide the foundations for inquiry-based science.

The second and third sections are more practical and personal in tone. The second section contains a chapter about what an inquiry-based lesson needs to contain and a chapter giving a simple example of an inquiry-based lesson using pendulums. Hopefully after reading the theory these chapters will show you what an inquiry-based science lesson actually looks like.

The third section goes onto provide practical methods and ideas of use in the classroom. Chapter 6 provides different methods and techniques that can be used in inquiry teaching. Chapters about teacher questioning, classroom management, evaluation and assessment, and why teachers might be reluctant to use inquiry are also provided.

There are many different ways of teaching inquiry and some of these different ways are shown in the final section. Here you can find a chapter about how to convert existing non-inquiry activities into inquiry-based ones, a chapter about more long-term inquiry work and a chapter looking at the different ways of doing science. The section ends with a list of possible title ideas for inquiry lessons you can use to develop your own lessons.

PREFACE

I studied biology at university and as part of my studies I had to take courses in plant biology, an essential topic for any biology student. The professor who lectured me on this subject was an old man nearing retirement. He would stride into class with a heavy volume about plant biology he had written about 40 years previously. His lectures consisted of opening his book at the desired chapter and reading aloud from it for the duration of the lecture. At the end of each session he would instruct us to read to the end of that chapter for 'homework' thus allowing him to start another chapter in the next lecture.

It is now some time since I left university. I can remember embarrassingly little about plant biology. I cannot name the main groupings of plants. I have a fuzzy recollection of plant physiology. I struggle to explain basic processes that occur in plants. In short I did not learn about plant biology well enough at university. The way in which I learnt was not motivating or interesting enough to make me remember what I had been taught, or to prompt me to do further independent study.

When I decided to write this book I immediately remembered my experience at university, and wanted to use this chance to make sure that other students, at whatever level, were taught in a more stimulating and engaging way than I had been then. Inquiry-based science offers students that chance. Instead of being passive learners in which information is stored, the student become the doer in the classroom, the one who is expected to work out what is happening and the one who must make the decisions. In such a way students remember what they learn best, not just tomorrow or the day after, but for years or decades.

Mark Walker

SECTION:

THE THEORY BEHIND INQUIRY-BASED SCIENCE

1

WHAT IS INQUIRY-BASED SCIENCE?

I keep the subject of my inquiry constantly before me, and wait till the first dawning opens
gradually, by little and little, into a full and clear light.

Isaac Newton

Inquiry: an old meaning revived

What does the word inquiry mean to you? If you look it up in a dictionary, you will probably see
that it means the posing of questions, the finding out of something, the searching out of
information, or the carrying out of an investigation. This last meaning is the one this book
concentrates on: inquiry as a form of investigation.

The word inquiry used to be used to describe what scientists did when they were finding things
out about the world and conducting experiments. The way in which scientists worked was known
as a whole 'inquiry.' The quote from Isaac Newton that is given at the beginning of this chapter
is an example of this old usage. Today we rarely call the work scientists do 'inquiry', preferring
other more modern words such as 'research,' 'investigation' or 'study'. The word inquiry seems
old fashioned and stuffy.

But inquiry in its traditional meaning has made a come back and has been used to describe a
modern method of teaching science known as inquiry-based science. In inquiry-based science
instead of simply being lectured about what they need to know or being told how to conduct
experiments by teachers this method of teaching forces students to do what scientists have always
had to do when they wanted to find something new and that is to actually do an investigation
themselves.

What is inquiry-based science?

Scientists study the natural world. They try to answer questions about the world around them. When conducting research scientists use a number of skills. These skills are called the science process skills. They include observation, description, question finding, planning of experiments, prediction, and experimentation (NRC 1996). Scientists use these skills in a methodical sequence. One such sequence, and the most well known is the 'scientific method,' but there are others. Scientists also possess certain attitudes and beliefs that they have when using these skills and methods. Altogether these different factors make up scientific inquiry; this is what scientists are doing when they are conducting research. Scientific inquiry is actually a good name for the work that scientists do, because when conducting science scientists are trying to find the answers to questions and problems they have and they are inquiring in a scientific way.

Inquiry-based science is a teaching method in which students work in a similar way as scientists when they are doing research. In inquiry-based science the students formulate their own questions, create hypotheses, and design investigations that test these hypotheses and answer the question proposed (NRC 1996, NRC 2000). The work students do in inquiry-based science mirrors the work which scientists do when they are conducting research. To put it simply the students work as 'junior scientists.'

It is important to recognize the differences between inquiry-based science and non-inquiry forms of science teaching. Simply by having students 'do an experiment' does not mean they are engaged in inquiry-based science. In a typical non-inquiry lesson the teacher would explain the important points of the topic being learnt, then the students would be given an experiment to do to reinforce this knowledge. The students would be given a worksheet explaining what methods they had to follow to complete the experiment, and maybe even be told what results they were expected to find. Everything would be written up in a lab book as a lab report at the end of the lesson. A professional scientist working in a research laboratory does not work in such a way.

A lesson taught using inquiry-based methods is very different. The teacher would introduce the topic in some way maybe with a demonstration or by showing the students some interesting phenomenon. Maybe the teacher would pose a problem about the topic to the students, or maybe if the students are advanced enough the teacher could guide the students to find a problem on their own. The students would then be expected to formulate a question about the problem; from this question they would develop a hypothesis. Instead of being given a worksheet, or a detailed list of instructions to follow the students would be expected to develop a method themselves. After the experiment the students would be expected to decide if their initial hypothesis was correct or not and then to try to solve the problem. They are doing more than simply doing an experiment they are working like real scientists.

Inquiry-based learning reflects modern practices within pedagogical science. The constructivist theory of learning is embedded within the idea of inquiry-based learning. This is because the inquiry-based learning idea is based upon how scientists work and scientists themselves work in a constructivist way. This convenient dovetailing of science, science education, and constructivism results in a teaching method that combines the strengths of each discipline. To fully understand inquiry-based science is it necessary therefore to understand the basic principles of science research and the ideas and theory behind constructivism. These topics will be discussed in later chapters. If at this stage inquiry-based science seems very complicated and difficult to understand, and you cannot see how you could teach using it, do not despair! This chapter is only meant to act as a general introduction, the ideas and principles behind inquiry will hopefully become clearer once you have read later chapters and seen some examples.

What are the advantages of using inquiry-based science?

There are two main advantages of teaching science through inquiry. Firstly by using the process of inquiry students remember and understand scientific knowledge better. Secondly while using inquiry students learn how scientists generate knowledge and how the current body of scientific knowledge was developed and produced (Schwab 1962). Once students have learnt how scientific knowledge is produced they can then go on to use the same skills and processes to generate new knowledge for themselves.

Inquiry-based methods of teaching improve student achievement at science. Studies from the early 1980s showed that students who were exposed to science lessons with more hands-on practical work obtained higher test scores and had better science process skills than counterparts taught using more traditional methods (Shymansky 1983, Bredderman 1982, Shymansky et al 1982, Shymansky et al. 1990, Haury 1993). These results are confirmed in more recent studies, which have found that students with teachers who use specific aspects of inquiry in their lesson do better at standard testing (von Secker & Lissitz 1999, von Secker 2002). Students introduced to inquiry study receive higher test marks (Marx et al. 1998, Cuevas et al. 2003).

Apart from increasing achievement levels of students, inquiry-based science also has a positive effect on students' attitudes towards science. Students engaged in inquiry-orientated work find science more interesting and exciting, and had a more positive view of science (Kyle et al. 1986, Gibson & Chase 2002). Generally speaking there is a fall in interest in science amongst students as they enter and proceed through secondary school, and the use of more inquiry-based science, which students see as being more relevant could be a way of combating this (Gibson & Chase 2002).

‚Traditional' ways of teaching science

In the early 1960s it was recognized that the teaching of science in schools was not being effective at producing scientifically literate individuals. There was a perceived danger that as a result of this the U.S. could lag behind other leading powers in science and technological advances. The teaching of science content was seen as the predominant aim of science, and lessons were based to a large extent on textbook reading and exercises. This 'traditional' way of teaching science was well described by Costenson & Lawson (1986):

> "…teaching centered around one fact-laden text, and consisted of assign, recite, test, and then, discuss the test."

This so called 'traditional' way of teaching science emphasized the knowledge of scientific facts, laws, theories and their uses. Laboratory activities were only used as a way of verifying science concepts previously learnt (Costenson & Lawson 1986, Shymansky 1984). Lessons involved students listening to teacher lectures on the topic being studied and readings from set textbooks.

Inquiry as a modern method of teaching science

In response to these failings a number of reform programs and new teaching ideas were introduced. These were based on the idea of inquiry, basically that students should be involved in the asking and solving of questions in science lessons (Chiappetta, 1997). Examples of these early schemes included the Biological Sciences Curriculum Study (BSCS 1970) and the Science As A Process Approach (American Association for the Advancement of Science (AAAS 1975). These schemes emphasized an understanding of the nature of science and science as a process. Laboratory exercises were seen as an integral part of science learning and not just as a confirmation activity at the end of a lesson. Scientific educators such as Schwab (1962), Herron (1971), Tamir (1985) and Welch at al. (1981) all promoted the teaching of science using inquiry like ideas. Such ideas were not new and had first been proposed in the late 19th and early 20th centuries by a number of philosophers, most notably John Dewey (1933) but at the time had failed to be implemented widely.

The reforms of the mid 1960s and 1970s can be seen as the forerunners of today's inquiry-based science, and they share many features of today's inquiry-based science. Unfortunately although these reforms received wide support from science educationalists, like the ideas of Dewey earlier in the century, they failed to be widely implemented in schools. Teaching of science in schools for the most part continued to follow the traditional pattern (Costenson & Lawson 1986).

Once again the failings of science education that was based on the traditional format came to the fore with the publication of the A Nation at Risk report in 1983. This report again highlighted the poor standards of teaching in many of the U.S.'s schools, and suggested that students should gain an introduction to the methods of scientific inquiry and reasoning while at school. The idea of inquiry-based science was further developed and encompassed many of the ideas of the previous reform efforts.

The Science for all Americans and Benchmarks for Scientific Literacy reports

These two documents provided the basis of the later National Standards in Science Education and its emphasis on learning science through inquiry. The first of these documents, Science for all Americans, was published in 1990 and focused on the need for improved scientific literacy. The report highlights the fact that content laden curricula do not necessarily improve student's level of scientific literacy and that a greater emphasis on understanding was needed. Science is divided into a number of chapters showing that learning and understanding about the common elements of science and the interrelatedness of scientific disciplines is more important that factual knowledge in any one subject area.

These themes were continued in the 1993 Benchmarks for Scientific Literacy. This document took the ideas proposed in the Science for all Americans document and provided learning goals for students of science at different stages of their education. As the Benchmarks made clear they were not designed to be used as a curriculum, and they do not tell teachers which teaching methods to use or what exactly to teach. The Benchmarks simply provide a set of science goals; things students should know and be able to do. The idea was that Benchmarks could be used by teachers to build their own curriculum using teaching methods they felt comfortable with. It was hoped that this flexibility would encourage teachers to use varied methods of teaching, not simply 'chalk and talk' or inquiry-based, but rather a good mixture of teaching practices and ones suited to the topics they had to teach.

Scientific inquiry, what science is and how it is conducted, was given especial emphasis making up the first chapter, entitled 'the nature of science' of both Science for all Americans and the Benchmarks. The National Science Education Standards that were published 3 years later was heavily influenced by the ideas proposed in these two documents. However, the main thrust of the National Science Education Standards was that science was an activity best learnt and understood through the use of inquiry-based science.

The National Science Education Standards

Inquiry-based science really took center stage in the mid 1990s, with the publication of the National Science Education Standards (NRC 1996), a key document guiding science education in the United States of America. The idea of inquiry and inquiry-based science was interwoven into this document, and this method was stated as being the best way of teaching science to our children. Inquiry was defined as:

> 'the diverse ways in which scientists study the natural world and propose explanations based on evidence derived from their work. Inquiry also refers to the activities of students in which they develop knowledge and understanding of scientific ideas, as well as an understanding of how scientists study the natural world.'

The first part of this statement considers inquiry as being how scientists conduct science; as mentioned this is commonly known as scientific inquiry. The second part of the definition considers inquiry as how students learn science and learn about how scientists work. This is best done through inquiry-based learning, as the standards make clear when they say that:

> 'Inquiry is a multifaceted activity that involves making observations; posing questions; examining books and other sources of information to see what is already known; planning investigations; reviewing what is already known in the light of experimental evidence; using tools to gather, analyze, and interpret data; proposing answers, explanations, and predictions; and communicating the results. Inquiry requires identification of assumptions, use of critical and logical thinking, and consideration of alternative explanations.'

The best way for students to learn how to do science and to learn about how scientists think is to actually use the same skills and methods as scientists use in scientific inquiry. This is the central tenet behind inquiry-based science, getting students to work like scientists.

The National Science Education Standards emphasized the importance of getting students to generate their own questions to investigate, ones based on their pre-existing knowledge and experience. The standards make clear that the student and not the teacher should initiate this process:

> 'Inquiry into authentic questions generated from student experiences is the central strategy for teaching science.'

A further report by the NRC, entitled 'Inquiry and the national science education standards: A guide for teaching and learning' (NRC 2000) further extended the ideas presented in the NSES and provided 5 essential features which inquiry should contain;

- Learners are engaged by scientifically orientated questions.

- Learners give priority to evidence, which allows them to develop and evaluate explanations that address scientifically orientated questions.

- Learners formulate explanations from evidence to address scientifically orientated questions.

- Learners evaluate their experiences in the light of alternative explanations, particularly those reflecting scientific understanding.

- Learners communicate and justify their proposed explanations.

A comparison between a non-inquiry and an inquiry-based science activity

Below are two different activities to teach the same topic: the factors that affect photosynthesis in pondweed. The first activity is not inquiry-based and is a fairly typical example of the experiments commonly conducted in school science lessons. The second activity is more inquiry-based and possesses many of the features seen in an inquiry-based lesson. In this experiment students are not told what to do but are expected to decide for themselves how to conduct the experiment and how to collect results. These two different methods of teaching the same topic are given here to provide a comparison between inquiry and non-inquiry methods, and to try to help you understand the differences between the two. Although the experiments are most suitable for older students of about 9th grade onwards, the principles behind an inquiry-based lesson and the differences between the activities are valid for experiments at every age range.

Non-inquiry activity:

Germination is dependant on temperature

Background Information:
Germination is the beginning of planned and systematic growth of a seed. Just like many other life processes germination is affected by the temperature. In chemical reactions inside living things the speed of reactions increases with increasing temperatures. However, the temperature required for germination to begin can vary greatly depending on the species of plant. Every species has its own optimal temperature for germination to start.

Material:
2 Petri dishes, a thermometer, garden cress seeds, a large clear plastic container kept damp, a fridge.

Time	Number of germinated seeds	
	Room temperature	4 °C
24 hours		
3 days		
1 week		
2 weeks		

Questions
What influence does raising the temperature have on germination?
Why do seeds germinate faster when it is warmer?
List 3 factors, which seeds need in order to germinate.

This non-inquiry activity:

- Has a stated goal. Both in the title and in the introduction section the information the student is expected to learn is stated clearly: Germination is influenced by temperature. In this activity the students must only confirm this statement.

- A detailed list of instructions is given in the method section. The student only has to follow the method in order to correctly complete the practical.

- The students do not have to think independently in order to answer the questions. Students must simply regurgitate information contained within the text.

In a non-inquiry exercise such as this one, background information would be provided to the students before they conducted the experiment. For example here some information is given on the worksheet before the instructions for the experiment are given. Sometimes the teacher would give a short lecture to the students providing the background information, or even give them some textbook reading to do before they began the experiment. This background information would contain information about what they were expected to find in the experiment. The student's task would simply be to try to confirm what they had been told or had read when doing the experiment.

Often at the end of non-inquiry experiments, such as this one, students are asked to answer questions using the information they were given before the activity began or which could be found in standard school textbooks. These questions are therefore not questions testing understanding, but rather testing how students knowledge and remembering skills.

Inquiry-based science activity:

Imagine that you work as a scientist in a biological research lab. One day your boss comes to you with a problem he wants you to answer:

'Global warming could be a big problem for farmers all around the world. The germination of some species of plants could be affected. Design an experiment to find out how global warming could affect seed germination in the spring, and if this will be a problem for farmers'.

You have to design and conduct an experiment to find out what effect global warming could have on seed germination. You should:
- Decide which experiments to conduct
- Decide which data to collect
- Do the experiment
- Make a poster showing your results and conclusions

Questions
Which other factors apart from temperature affect germination? How would you conduct an experiment to find out what effect these other factors have on germination?

Your boss gives you a chemical that is able to remove the oxygen from the air. How could you design an experiment to find out if germinating seeds need oxygen? Draw a diagram of how you would set up the experiment.

The more inquiry-based activity:

- The students are not told what the expected results are. Students are simply told to investigate how global warming affects plant growth. In a non-inquiry experiment students might be told that 'higher temperatures caused by global warming will cause plants to photosynthesize more'.

- The students must decide themselves how to set up the experiment and which method to use.

- There is no table for the students to fill in their results.

- The students have to think in order to answer the questions. They not simply copy the answers from their worksheet. The questions ask them how they would conduct further experiments and prompt them to think about new problems, and not simply ask for pieces of knowledge.

This activity forces the students to think much more than the first one. Students do not simply follow the instruction sheet but must decide what to do themselves. They have to plan, design and conduct the experiment themselves. The student has to decide which data to collect, and what it actually means.

Notice that in this activity no background information is given. In an inquiry-based activity the teacher does not provide background information or textbook reading. In an inquiry-based exercise the students are expected to find out for themselves what the result of the experiment is and what it means. The students do not simply confirm information they have already been given, but must find the information for themselves.

Classifying inquiry-based science

There have been numerous attempts at defining and classifying inquiry-based science (Anderson 2002). Inquiry-based science can cover a wide range of different types of activities with varying levels of openness, so it is important to have some way of classifying inquiry lesson and deciding how inquiry like they are.

Schwab and Herron's scale of laboratory openness

Schwab was one of the first science educators to develop the concept of inquiry-based science. He wanted to make laboratory work more like real scientific experimentation. His book 'The teaching of science as enquiry' (Schwab, 1962) paved the way for the development of inquiry-based science in the 1970s. Schwab was the first to try to classify inquiry. He recognized three levels of inquiry science. In his first level the teacher posed a problem, which students then tried to answer by using different methods. In the second level the teacher posed a problem, but this time the students had to develop a method themselves. In the third level of inquiry the students had to both pose the problem and develop a suitable method.

Herron later extended and refined this way of looking at inquiry. He developed what is known as the Schwab-Herron Scale of Laboratory Openness (Herron 1971). This possessed an additional level of inquiry, and could be expressed in tabular form. This shows who should provide or do what in a laboratory exercise. An example of this scale is provided below.

Level	Problem	Method	Results
0	Given	Given	Given
1	Given	Given	Student
2	Given	Student	Student
3	Student	Student	Student

Structured, guided and open inquiry

Tafoya et al. (1980) produced a simple method of classifying inquiry, depending on who provided the question on which a lesson was based upon. This is based on Schwab and Herron's ideas, but is expressed in written form and not tabular. Inquiry was divided into structured, guided or open. This method of classifying inquiry was easy to understand and easy to use and has found wide acceptance.

Inquiry-based science lessons can be either:

- **Open:** The lesson is wholly inquiry-based. The students decide on the problem and question to investigate and the method to use to answer it.

- **Guided:** In guided inquiry the teacher provides the question that needs to be answered. The students decide on the best method in which to answer this question.

- **Structured:** In structured inquiry the teacher provides the students both with the question to be answered and the method to use to answer it, but not the expected outcome. The only difference between structured inquiry and confirmation exercises is that in structured inquiry the student does not know the outcome of the experiment.

- **Confirmation Exercises:** these are not inquiry-based at all. In confirmation exercises the teacher tells the students what the solution is to the question at the beginning of the lesson, and then gives instructions of how to conduct an experiment to confirm this.

These different categories of inquiry can be seen as being analogous to Schwab and Herron's levels of inquiry, with confirmation exercises being at inquiry level 0, and open inquiry being at level 3. Here is an example of how an activity about the rate of photosynthesis in pondweed, could be taught with these different grades of inquiry:

- **Open**: Students are told to 'investigate the factors which affect the rate of photosynthesis in pondweed'.

- **Guided inquiry:** Students are told to design and conduct an experiment to answer the following question 'how does light intensity affect the rate of photosynthesis in pondweed?'

- **Structured inquiry:** Students are told 'how does light intensity affect the rate of photosynthesis in pondweed? Collect a lamp, a beaker, and a sprig of pondweed, and set the experiment up as in the diagram provided. Observe how many bubbles of air come from the pondweed each minute when the lamp is at 10, 20 and 30 cm distance from the pondweed. Fill in this table.'

- **Confirmation exercise:** Students are told 'the rate of photosynthesis is greater at higher light intensities. You will see this in the following experiment. Collect a lamp, a beaker, and a sprig of pondweed, and set the experiment up as in this diagram. Observe how many bubbles of air come from the pondweed each minute when the lamp is at 10, 20 and 30 cm distance from the pondweed. Fill in this table. As you can see more bubbles of air are produced when the lamp is closer to the pondweed.'

Inquiry as a continuum

The classification of inquiry-based science lessons into structured, guided or open inquiry is relatively simple to understand. However, if teachers are only introduced to this method of classifying inquiry there is the danger that they fail to see the connections between the different forms of inquiry. With this method it is difficult to see how non-inquiry lessons could be made into inquiry ones or how structured activities could be changed into open inquiry activities. The advantage of Schwab and Herron's Scale of Laboratory Openness is that it is clear that inquiry is a scale, and where you are on the scale depends on who does what in the classroom.

Maybe a better, but more complex way of looking at inquiry is to use an inquiry matrix, such as the one shown below which has been developed by Fradd et al (2002), and Sutman et al (1998). This matrix is based on the ones developed by Herron and Schwab but it splits inquiry up into more stages. Whereas in open, guided, structured method of classifying inquiry the different stages of inquiry appear to be discrete entities, in the matrix it is more obvious that inquiry occurs over a continuum. Lessons belong on a scale of 0 to 5, and can be made more or less open by changing who is responsible for certain components of the lesson. The lesson is broken down into several components, from questioning to applying, and the decisions in each of these stages is made by either the teacher or the student.

Inquiry Level	Questioning	Planning	Implementing	Concluding		Reporting	Applying
			Carrying out plan	Analyze Data	Draw Conclusions		
0	Teacher	Teacher	Teacher	Teacher	Teacher	Teacher	Teacher
1	Teacher	Teacher	Students /Teacher	Teacher	Teacher	Students	Teacher
2	Teacher	Teacher	Students	Students / Teacher	Students/ Teacher	Students	Teacher
3	Teacher	Students /Teacher	Students	Students	Students	Students	Students
4	Students/ Teacher	Students	Students	Students	Students	Students	Students
5	Students	Students	Students	Students	Students	Students	Students

The matrix makes clear that the openness of a lesson is determined by the balance between the teacher and the student's responsibilities. The more decisions that the student has to make the more open the lesson becomes. With the inquiry matrix it is easier for teachers to understand how they can make lessons more open.

SCIENTIFIC INQUIRY:
HOW SCIENTISTS WORK

Science is facts; just as houses are made of stones, so is science made of facts; but a
pile of stones is not a house and a collection of facts is not necessarily science.

Henri Poincaré

If in inquiry-based science students learn using the same methods and ideas as scientists, it is
essential that any teacher wishing to teach using inquiry-based science understand what these
methods and ideas are. So what is scientific inquiry? Unfortunately many people, including
teachers, do not understand how science works or how science is conducted. Science is often
perceived as being a mysterious secret activity, which only a restricted few made up of the very
eccentric or very intelligent (and mostly male) are allowed to take part in.

If we are to encourage more people to take an interest in science it is important that they learn
that science is open to everyone and is in fact very simple to do. Today's world is technology and
science rich, but science also provides modern day problems, such as global warming and stem
cell research. Citizens have to comprehend science if they are to make informed choices about
how our world should look in the future and to fully take part in today's society (Bentley et al.
1999).

What is science made up of?

Science can be considered as containing three main facets (Koch 2000):

- The Scientific Process: Scientists use a number of skills when conducting science and
  these are known as the Science Process Skills. Scientists use these skills in a methodical
  manner, often known as the Scientific Method.

- Scientific Knowledge: The Scientific Process Skills and the Scientific Method are used by scientists to produce knowledge, ideas and concepts. These are commonly formulated as hypotheses, theories and laws.

- Scientific Attitudes and Values: Different scientists might work in different ways or believe in different things, but they still have shared values and attitudes. Science contains a number of key values.

These three things combine together to form something known as the 'nature of science.' Explained simply this is the way in which science is done and the qualities it possesses.

The Scientific Process

Science process skills

While following the 'Scientific Method' or one of the other methods of conducting science, scientists have to use a number of different skills and techniques. These skills are known generally as the 'science process skills.' It is important to remember that these skills are transferable. They are not exclusively used by scientists, but are of importance in a number of different activities unrelated to science. What makes the science process skills special is that scientists use them in a specific manner and specific sequence. The following list of process skills is one developed by the Science - A Process Approach (SAPA) program run by the American Association for the Advancement of Science (1975). They considered two kinds of process skills, the basic process skills and the integrated process skills.

The Basic Science Process Skills:
- **Observation:** Maybe the simplest but most important skill. Scientists must be able to use their senses to observe the world around them.

- **Classifying:** The grouping and ordering of objects into categories.

- **Measuring:** describing the specific dimensions of an object or event.

- **Communication:** this is the describing of an object or event that has been observed to others.

- **Inferring:** this is the drawing of a conclusion for why something occurs, based on collected data.

- **Predicting:** the making of an educated guess about some future event, based on what we have already seen.

As can be seen these skills are all related to each other and are the beginning steps of conducting a scientific investigation. Each skill merges fairly easily into the next.

The Integrated Science Process Skills:

- **Controlling variables:** being able to identify variables and then control all but one is an important part of conducting science.

- **Defining operationally:** this is the identification of the measurements to be used in the experiments. How often will you measure? What will be measured?

- **Formulating hypotheses:** this is similar to making a prediction. What is the expected outcome of the experiment?

- **Collecting data:** the gathering of information in a systematic way.

- **Interpreting of data:** the organization, analysis and interpretation of information.

- **Experimenting:** the designing of an experiment to test some hypothesis.

- **Making models:** the use of information to make a simulation of some event or observation.

These integrated skills lead on from the basic skills and as can be seen they are more complex and difficult. Because it is becoming increasingly important that students learn how to do science and not just learn facts about science it is important to teach the science process skills to students. This division into basic and integrated skills takes into account the different abilities of students at different age ranges (AAAS 1975). The primary process skills are designed to be mastered by children at the elementary of lower primary level, while the integrated skills are aimed more at children at a middle or high school level. The integrated science process skills build and develop on the primary skills. This division into primary and integrated skills reflects the Piagetian cognitive development model that will be discussed in the next chapter.

As middle or high school teachers these integrated process skills will probably be of most interest to you as these are the skills you will wish to get your students to learn. However, although the students you will be teaching will already have some mastery of the basic process skills, there is always scope for improvement. Inquiry-based science offers you the chance to get students to use a range of these skills.

The Scientific Method

When scientists work they follow a simple procedure or number of steps. This is generally known as the 'scientific method'. Generally agreed upon steps of the scientific method are:

- **Observation and Description:** The first step is to observe and describe something. Scientists tend to be good at noticing the world around them. This stage can include the keeping of notes, describing objects or processes, or even simply reading what others already know. Scientists spend a lot of time studying and reading to improve their knowledge and to learn what other scientists have already done.

22

- **Questioning**: After observing and describing something the scientist discovers a problem. This is normally expressed in the form of a question.

- **Hypothesis formulation**: A hypothesis is developed to explain what has been observed and described. The scientist tries to identify an answer to the question he has just formulated.

- **Predicting**: The hypothesis is then used to predict what could happen in a certain situation.

- **Experimenting**: Next an experiment is conducted to see if the predicted results are obtained. This is known as the testing of the hypothesis. Normally in an experiment variables are identified and all but one is controlled. All the variables are kept the same apart from the one being investigated. Experiments have to be replicated many times to make sure reliable results are obtained.

- **Conclusion**: The results of the experiment are used to see if they support the hypothesis. If so then the hypothesis can be accepted, if not then the hypothesis has been shown to be wrong. New problems and questions to investigate are generated at this stage.

Is there really a 'Scientific Method'?

But is there really a scientific method? Is there really a single way of creating scientific knowledge? The simple answer is no. There is no single, step-by-step method of 'doing science,' to try to produce one is an oversimplification. There are many various ways of conducting science that do not necessarily follow the steps given above.

Different kinds of scientists working in different fields work in different ways. The way a chemist works in the lab with chemicals is very different from how a geologist works in the field looking at fossils, or how a meteorologist studies the weather at the North Pole.

Even scientists working in the same field will use different steps and different methods and work in different orders. 'Lets change this and see what happens' is an equally valid, and much used way of conducting science used by scientists which does not follow the steps of the scientific method given above. Maybe it would be better if the term 'scientific methods' was used instead to encompass these different ways of working.

This does not necessarily mean that the concept and steps of the scientific method are useless. To have the term scientific method is useful because it provides a broad generalization of what scientists do and helps to explain the process of science in a simple way. It is a good starting point to start learning about science and trying to understand how science works. It creates a certain amount of order and structure, which can be a useful starting point for school learners to have. Some of the other methods of conducting science are given below. Although the methods of teaching inquiry given in this book often follow the traditional steps of the scientific method, please bear in mind that real scientists do not necessarily work in this way.

Other ways of conducting science

Experimentation is the most well known method of conducting science, but it is not the only one. The following techniques are also ways of conducting science, and were described in detail by Bentley et al. (1999).

- **Trial and Error**: Although this might seem too random to be considered scientific, it is in fact an important scientific technique. Drug and pesticides companies test hundreds of different chemicals to find ones that work. New products are often not invented but rather found through calculated luck.

- **Product testing**: Many scientists are involved in testing things to see which ones work best. Think of the safety tests different brands of cars have to go through. Many things we use every day need to be tested.

- **Inventing**: When inventing scientists use their prior knowledge, but through the process of inventing they develop new ideas. Inventing is a bit like trial and error, in that if something does not work you try something different until it does work.

- **Making Models**: Models are made to show how something works when it is not possible to do or use the real thing. They are a form of simulation. It can include the making of physical models, such as making model planes to try to see how real ones will fly when they are built. But it can also include the making of mathematical or theoretical models that show how some process works, for example how animal populations change over time when the level of food available alters.

- **Documenting**: This is simply the keeping of records, often over long periods of time. A good example is meteorologists and weathermen, who observe and document the weather to study climate change. Another example would be ecologists who document how the species present in an ecosystem change over time.

Scientific knowledge

Scientists work to produce knowledge, ideas and concepts. These are usually formulated as hypothesis, theories or laws. Many non-scientists misunderstand what exactly hypotheses, theories and laws are, and this leads them to misinterpret the importance of scientific work. For example many people denounce evolution by saying 'it is just a theory', thinking that a theory is something non-proven, purely theoretical and untested. In colloquial speech the word 'theory' is often used to mean a simple guess. How many times have you heard someone say, "Well that's my theory" when they have made a guess for why something occurred. In fact for scientists a theory is something extremely robust that all the evidence shows is correct.

A **Hypothesis** is best described as being an 'educated guess'. From looking at some object, event or occurrence scientists predict what might happen next time the same thing happens. A hypothesis is the main driver of experimentation. Scientists conduct experiment to try to show whether hypotheses are correct or not.

A **Theory** is an explanation for a certain event, which is supported by many verified hypotheses. When scientists conduct an experiment many times and continually obtain the same result, they begin to develop a theory. This is the idea for why something occurs or happens. Correct hypothesizes can be considered as being the 'evidence' for this theory.

A **Scientific law** is something that is considered as being pretty much a 'fact.' The same thing happens every time and everywhere where you try it. They are always true, and no one has shown that they are not true. Famous scientific laws include the law of gravity and the law of thermodynamics. Laws tend to be simple and specific.

There is often a false belief that there is a step like progression between hypotheses, theories and laws. For example many people believe that theories that have been 'proved' well enough become laws. Laws are seen as being 'better' or more certain than theories. This is not actually the case. Laws and theories are not interchangeable. They are simply different kinds of scientific knowledge (Bredermann et al. 2002).

While a Scientific Law is relatively simple, a theory can be quite complex and made up of many separate parts. Although separate parts of a theory can be shown to be wrong, this does not mean the theory, as a whole is incorrect. Scientists work on making the many separate parts of a theory simpler or more encompassing. Scientists generally consider both theories and scientific laws as being true. If enough evidence is collected which does not fit into a theory, the old theory can be overturned and a new one developed. However this rarely happens, and theories tend to be extremely robust.

An important feature of a hypothesis and a theory is that they must be falsifiable. It must be possible that some new discovery or results from some experiment could show that a theory is incorrect. The statement 'there are no aliens' is a scientific statement, because it will be proved wrong if aliens come to visit one day. A statement that cannot be shown to be false is not scientific it is faith.

Scientific attitudes and values

Scientists have a set of values, beliefs and attitudes which influence how they think about science and how they conduct science. Perhaps the most basic of these is the belief that the universe is understandable and the way in which it functions can be discovered. By studying natural objects scientists believe they can discover patterns, relationships and rules which help them understand how the universe functions. There is a lively debate amongst scientific philosophers and scientists about what views and attitudes scientists have. There is no agreed upon list and different authors have different ideas. The following list is taken from Smith and Sharman (1999) and includes what most scientists would consider as important attributes of science.

- **Science is empirical:** Science relies upon observation and experiment. The word empirical means to experiment, and comes from the Greek word for a test or trial, it is related to the Latin word for experiment. Scientists use their senses to collect information about the environment around them using measurement. Knowledge is built from experimentation and experience.

- **Science is tentative:** Scientists make guesses about why certain things occur. Scientists do not prove anything. Old ideas can be shown to be wrong. There are no right answers. The knowledge developed by science is therefore not rigid, but can change and be altered with time.

- **Experiments can be repeated:** The experiments conducted by one scientist can be repeated by another scientist and similar results obtained. Replication of experiments helps to confirm whether conclusions are correct or not.

- **Science is falsifiable:** Scientific claims must be testable and be able to be shown to be false. Scientists must be able to collect data that supports or refutes a claim.

- **Science is self-correcting**: Repeated experimentation leads to the discovery of errors and their correction.

Some authors also argue that science is characterized by progress, that scientific knowledge is built upon and developed over time, but this is disputed (Lakatos 1970, Popper 1972). Others consider science as being heuristic, meaning that it is based upon assumptions and hypothesis Smith and Sharman (1999).

Scientist's value open-mindedness. Although all scientists conduct research with prior views scientists try to be objective and fair in the work that they do. Scientists consider that the process of developing ideas, designing experiments and forming explanations is a creative process. Scientists also value criticism. The work done by one scientist can be criticized by another. There is no one single authority within science, even if someone is an 'expert' this does not necessarily mean they are always right and can never be shown to be wrong.

The Nature of Science

As mentioned at the beginning of this chapter the skills and methods scientists use, their ideas and knowledge, and their views and attitudes all combine to form the Nature of Science, often referred to as NOS. The Nature of Science can be considered as being the sociology of science (Ledermann et al 2002, Chiappetta, Koballa, & Collette, 1998).

However, as should have become clear while reading this chapter it is difficult to form an exact definition of the Nature of Science because there is no correct or clear single way of defining each of its separate parts. Science is complex and dynamic. Different scientists have different ways of looking and thinking about what they do. Scientists in different disciplines consider how they work in different ways and use different methods. Scientists from different cultures will look at science from different viewpoints and with different values. This does not necessarily mean that any of these views of science are wrong, only different.

It has long been recognized that it is important that students gain a good understanding of the concepts behind the Nature of Science and learn about the Nature of Science as part of their science education. The AAAS (1993) and NRC (1996) emphasize the teaching of the Nature of Science in science lessons as an important part of understanding how science is conducted and what science means. However, many students, and teachers, have a poor understanding of the Nature of Science (Abd-El-Khalick & Lederman, 2000, Duschl, 1990).

An Example of scientific research

Sexual Selection in Widowbirds

The Swedish biologist Malte Andersson (1982) studied the ecology and biology of wildlife in East Africa. One species of bird, the Widowbird, caught his attention. The Widowbird is a small species of bird that lives on the east African Savannah. It is rather dull in coloration, but is quite distinctive because the males have very long tails. These tails can be over 70 cm in length. Females have only very short tails of about 10 cm in length. Male Widowbirds live in territories, and attract females by doing a characteristic jumping dance. If a female is attracted she enters his territory and makes a nest. Successful males can have half a dozen females in their territory.

Observation and Description: Andersson observed these birds and watched their habits. From his training and prior knowledge as a biologist he thought the long tails of the male Widowbirds could be caused because of sexual selection. Sexual selection is a special branch of natural selection. Whereas in natural selection those features are selected for which are most advantageous to the individuals survival, in sexual selection traits or features that make an individual appear more attractive to the opposite sex are favored. For example in an extinct species of deer, known as the Giant Irish Elk the females preferred to mate with males who had larger antlers. Over time males with larger and larger antlers gained more mating success and antlers became larger and larger. Antlers are a useful indicator of a male deer's strength, but sometimes females will choose traits that appear disadvantageous, such as the long tails in the Widowbirds. If a male Widowbird has a very long tail but is still good enough to survive, then he must be good to mate with!

Questioning/Hypothesis formulation: Do female Widowbirds prefer to mate with males with longer tails? Andersson thought that males with longer tails would have more female mates. But how could he show this? He had to think of an experiment to see if sexual selection was really happening.

Predicting: Andersson predicted that if he extended the tails of some males they would obtain more mates than males with shorter unaltered tails.

Experimenting: He found a group of male Widowbirds and divided them into four groups. In the first group he cut the tails of the males off so that they had short tails. In the second group he stuck on the bits of tail he had cut from the first group onto their tails, meaning that their tails were now much longer than before. The third and fourth groups were control groups. The third group was left without any interference. In the fourth group he cut off the tails of the males and then stuck them on again to see if cutting the tails made any difference to mating success.

Andersson observed how successful males were both before and after the experiment by counting how many females were present within their territory. He found that males which had their tails shortened had fewer females. Males who had had their tails lengthened were able to attract more females and did better than those with the short tails. In the control groups there was no difference in the number of females present from the beginning to the end of the experiment.

Conclusion: Andersson concluded that those males with longer tails were able to attract more females and breed more than males with shorter tails: this showed that sexual selection really did happen. This experiment remains one of the classic experiments done in behavioral ecology and is a good example of how scientists work.

Meeting scientists

Susan Cartwright's work on Neutrinos

Susan Cartwright works at the department of Physics and Astronomy at the University of Sheffield, England. She conducts research into particle physics, and is studying the properties of neutrinos, these are weakly interacting, almost massless particles produced in radioactive decay and other similar processes. Learning about these will help us understand why our universe is the way it is.

Author: How do you do your research?
SC: I work as part of a large international collaboration, with several hundred scientists from many countries including Japan, Korea, the USA, and Canada. We hope to send a beam of neutrinos generated on the east coast of Japan, not far from Tokyo, to a detector located under a mountain on Japan's west coast, a distance of 295 km. This detector already exists, but needs to be complemented by a "near detector" located close to the origin of the Beam. I am helping design and build this near detector. This work uses a very large set of C++ computer programs.

Author: How important is answering questions to you?
SC: All scientific research is "answering questions," though the questions range from the apparently trivial ("what is the melting point of this substance?") to the profound ("what is the geometry of the universe?"). I can't imagine a scientific research project that wasn't "answering questions" in this broad sense.

Author: What do you think makes a good scientist?
SC: Science is about answering questions. Scientists need to be able to pick good questions: at any given time in any given field, many lines of inquiry are open, and some will be much more fruitful than others. Really great scientists seem to have the ability to identify the fruitful ones.

Scientists also need curiosity about the world. Scientists need a constructively critical outlook; new results need to be subjected to adequate scrutiny. Patience is also important: Rome wasn't built in a day, and neither is the average experiment (our beam won't turn on until 2009, and we are very worried that we won't get the experiment finished in time).

Author: How did you get interested in science?
SC: I can't remember a time when I wasn't interested in science.

Author: What skills do you think it is important for scientists to have?
SC: Almost all scientists require good communications skills, both oral and written. It is essential to be able to write well. Most results are first reported orally at international conferences, so good oral presentation skills are also needed.

Most scientists require good IT skills. Particle physics is particularly computer-intensive. The physical sciences typically require high levels of mathematical Skill. Good knowledge of electronics is almost always useful in the physical sciences.

Author: Why is science rewarding?
SC: For the same reason that being a writer or artist is rewarding: It's a creative art. When you build an experiment or complete an analysis, you have created something unique and personal, even though a C++ program may not be a particularly aesthetically pleasing object!

A successful experiment increases our understanding of the world. Science is intellectually engaging - you get to use your knowledge and skills to develop something you can call your own.

Kim Worley's work on the Human Genome Project

Kim Worley is an Associate Professor working at the Human Genome Sequencing Center, in the Department of Molecular and Human Genetics, Baylor College of Medicine, Houston.

Author: What are you conducting research into?
KM: My area of supervision is bioinformatics, particularly genome assemblies. That is working with computers to analyze DNA sequence and features. We assemble genomes by evaluating the short (500 to 1,000 base pairs) sequences generated by the sequencing process in the lab for runs of identity that indicate that the pieces overlap and by using information about the relationship between two short pieces of sequence that were sequenced from the two ends of a single subclone.

Author: What do you hope to find out?
KM: Ultimately, we hope that our research will provide information about human health, disease, and biology. The genome sequence of organisms other than humans informs human biology, because sequences that are conserved between species over evolutionary time are important for their function.

Author: How do you do your research?
KM: We do a lot of sequence comparisons, using tools like BLAST and Crossmatch. We manipulate large numbers of sequence files (>38 million for the bovine assembly), and the large files with information about the sequence files.

Author: Do you try to answer 'questions' in your research?
KM: Our research primarily produces data that speeds the research of many other folks around the world. Researchers on a particular disease or gene can make years of progress in a week once genome sequence becomes available.

Author: Do you use the 'scientific method' when sequencing DNA?
KM: Yes and no. We try to understand how to improve genome sequencing and assembly - many of the questions there are hypothesis driven. But, our primary goal of sequencing many organisms is less hypothesis driven.

Author: What do you think makes a good scientist?
KM: A questioning mind, the will to follow through, and an ability to communicate.

Author: Is science cooperative?

KM: Absolutely. Large projects like ours require collaborations of many people here (200 in our lab), and researchers around the world to interpret the data.

Author: What skills do you use when doing research?

KM: Different types of science require different skills. The more skills you have the more you can bring different approaches to a problem to gain new insight. My experience in engineering gives me a different perspective on problems than people who trained in biology. People who work with yeast can approach different questions than people who work with human cancers, but they can combine their knowledge and gain insight into both.

Author: Why is science rewarding?

KM: Unlike many professions where image or spin is important, science is testable. In that way it approaches truth.

Author: How do you learn while doing science?

KM: By reading, talking with others, and experimenting.

Author: How did you learn to do science?

KM: By working with other scientists.

CONSTRUCTIVISM:
HOW CHILDREN LEARN

A teacher is one who makes himself progressively unnecessary.

Thomas Carruthers

At school were you ever taught how to learn? Or were you just expected to turn up and remember what the teacher said? A teacher's job is to get his or her students to learn. To be able to do this it is essential that teachers have a good understanding of how their students learn.

The Behaviorist view of learning

The method in which you were taught at school probably reflected a theory of learning known as behaviorism. The behaviorist view of learning was originated by the American psychologist J. B. Watson, and extended by B.F. Skinner. Behaviorists believe that learning has little to do with psychological changes, but instead learning is a behavioral change. When something is learnt the behavior of the individual alters and this change can be measured or observed in some way.

A key feature of Behaviorism is the theory of 'operant conditioning', which says that the reason we do something depended on the consequences of us doing that action in the past. If students are praised when they do well and complete some task correctly, when they have to do the task again in the future they will remember how to do the task and successfully complete it.

The idea of operant conditioning has important implications for how behaviorists believe people learn. Learning using behaviorist ideas emphasizes rote and drill learning where learning is repeated time and time again until the students can do or remember something. A typical example of an exercise promoting this idea of learning would be a student learning a foreign language by having to complete a text with gaps in it. When they have completed the task successfully they have learnt what is needed and achieved the goals of the lesson.

The Constructivist theory of learning

Over the past century a new theory of how people learn has been developed. This is known as the Constructivist theory of learning. Key features of Constructivism are:

- **Prior knowledge: Learners already have ideas and knowledge before they begin to learn:** A key difference between Constructivism and earlier theories of learning is that Constructivism acknowledges that learners begin the learning process with ideas and knowledge of their own. In Constructivism this prior knowledge is acknowledged and used as a base on which to construct further knowledge. Learners may also have 'misconceptions,' or incorrect ideas, and in Constructivism it is important that these misconceptions are recognized and then altered through the learning process.

- **Knowledge is constructed:** The key feature of Constructivism is that learners create their own ideas. Ideas and knowledge are not simply 'passed on' from teacher to student, instead each student has to create, construct or build their own understanding. The ideas that learners create fit onto their previous ideas. If new ideas will not fit with the learners previous ideas cognitive conflict occurs and the learner must change their preconceptions.

- **Learning is active:** Students actively construct knowledge as they learn. Active learning is promoted when students have to do something themselves, rather than simply being told what they need to know. Students learn best when they are engaged in concrete hands-on learning. Learners need to be able to do, to touch, to make, to discover.

- **Learning depends on the environment the learner is in:** Learning depends on both the social environment and the physical environment of the learner. Learning is a social activity. Students learn best when they see the relevance of what they are learning. What students learn must have some connection to the world in which they live and the things that they do everyday.

The Constructivist theory of learning has important implications for how teachers help their students to learn. If these points are considered carefully it will be seen that they result in a different role for the teacher than that which is traditionally perceived. Normally teachers are seen as being a 'passer on' of knowledge. Students enter the classroom to be given knowledge by the teacher. A 'good' teacher is one who knows a lot about his or her subject.

Teachers in a constructivist setting instead of 'teaching,' have to get their students to learn themselves and construct knowledge independently. They have to find ways to get students to learn actively in a hands-on way. A teacher in such a setting is more of a mentor than a teacher. Teachers do not need to know about the topic being explored, instead it is more important that they are able to animate students to ask questions which are suitable for research, reflect on the experimental design, and decide whether data has been collected and analyzed in a suitable way. Teachers cannot be experts on every topic, and do not need to be to teach in an open or inquiry manner. The teacher and the students explore a topic together.

We all try to build up ideas and understanding to explain the things around us. Sometimes we are right in our ideas, but sometimes we are not. Children are no exceptions to this, they also try to think of reasons for the things they see, and these ideas can also be false. Education specialists call these false ideas 'misconceptions.' Consider this following example from Harlen (2004):

"The teacher explained the appearance of dew on grass on a cold morning in terms of water vapor in the air. The girl already had an explanation for this; her own idea that the coldness of the grass created the water. This idea also fitted her experience of the water drops on a bottle just after it was taken from the fridge. "

One of the goals of the teacher is to find out which misconceptions their students have, and to try to correct them. However this can be difficult. A child will retain his or her ideas; if they believe that they make better sense than the explanations they are given by the teacher (Harlen 2004). Children may remember explanations given to them by their teacher but have no real understanding of them, and thus may cling to their own misconceptions. Learners can be extremely reluctant to change misconceptions (Carin et al. 2005).

The process where a student is confronted with evidence that contradicts misconceptions and has to decide on a new explanation is known as conceptual change. For conceptual change to occur students have to become dissatisfied with their expositing idea, and the new idea must be more plausible and understandable. Teachers need to challenge students to consider different explanations and to discard misconceptions (Carin et al. 2005). Conceptual change is an important part of cognitive development.

A 'traditional' and Constructivist classroom compared

The best way to show the difference between a constructivist and 'traditional' classroom is to actually give examples of teachers teaching in these different ways.

As part of a course about how to teach inquiry Julie, one of our student teachers, had to give a sample lesson to a small class of middle school students. She had decided to teach about how mice learn to use mazes. She taught in what could be described as being a very 'traditional' way, even though we did not want her to. She stood at the front of the class, and dominated the lesson. She began by lecturing the students about mice biology and behavior, introducing such concepts as operant learning and trial and error and writing important words on the board. The students sat in rows and listened, seemingly attentively.

Next the students were allowed to do practical work. Real, live mice were available for use as was a maze made out of toy building blocks. The idea was that the students would see that the mice learnt by trial and error to find there way out of the maze. The students were carefully instructed how to put the mice in the maze and what they had to observe. After the students had done this they were told to write what they had found as an experimental write up in their lab books. Unfortunately the practical was not very successful. Mice maybe are not the most cooperative of lab animals! The students were disappointed. 'We didn't get the right answer!'

Although Julie thought she was teaching in a constructivist way, she was in fact not. She had provided the students with information at the beginning of the lesson, and then tried to get them confirm this by getting them to conduct an experiment. She decided on which method to use, not the students. The students own questions caused problems for Julie; she had only prepared what she wanted them to learn. Students asked questions like 'What sex are the mice?' 'How can you tell?' 'Do mice like water?' 'Do mice smell the way round the maze?' To these questions Julie had no answer and became embarrassed, and simply tried to divert the students onto another question, or told them that was not what they were meant to be studying! Maybe a more experienced teacher would have said 'I don't know, lets try to find out!'

Sarah, however did things very differently and in a much more constructivist way when she had to teach a similar class. She decided that she wanted to teach the class about the sense of taste. Unlike Julie she started the class differently, although the students instinctively sat in rows as they came into class, she moved from the front to be actually in the middle of the students. Instead of simply lecturing, she began by eating a banana, and then asking the class 'Why does a banana taste like a banana? Why does it not taste of something else?' This became the focus for a small class discussion, in which Sarah simply asked questions and let students express what ideas they had.

The practical example Sarah used was more inquiry-based than the one used by Julie. Sarah provided the students with an investigation question to start them off; 'What effect does your sense of smell have on your sense of taste?' The students then had to develop a way of answering this problem themselves. Sarah, prompted the class by asking them questions like, 'What do you think will happen when you can't smell?' 'Why?' 'Have you ever actually tested that?' 'How could you do that?' The students were responsible for designing the experiment themselves, and at the end, they told Sarah what they had found. The students set up an experiment where one student was blindfolded and then fed different types of food. They had to guess what food it was. Next, the student had a peg put on their nose, and had to re-taste everything and guess again. The students found that it was more difficult to guess when you had a peg on your nose. Not an ideal experiment, but at least student designed! Once the students had given their findings, Sarah gave the students a short worksheet with further information and questions for homework. As the students read this, one exclaimed 'I know all this, we have just learnt it!' In comparison to Julie's lesson the information came at the end and not at the beginning.

These examples show the main difference in the classroom when you follow constructivist ideas. Basically in a constructivist classroom and a traditional classroom you have different aims. The aim of a constructivist classroom is that students understand. In a traditional classroom the main aim is that students collect as much information as possible. This difference in aim leads to different ways of dealing with the curriculum and organizing lessons.

Traditionally based lessons tend to stick rigidly to the curriculum or teaching plan. Julie had a meticulous lesson plan, which was well planned, and conscientiously made, but it fell to pieces because it tried to teach too much and did not consider students desire to answer different questions. Julie simply wanted to teach her facts. This is in line with many traditional curricula, which want to cover as many different topic areas as possible to allow students to obtain the broadest possible knowledge possible and to learn the most important facts in every area.

Constructivist teachers consider the learning of facts as a secondary aim. Facts can be found simply from looking in a book. Sarah concentrated on getting students to understand a relatively small idea; that your nose plays a large role in your sense of taste. She could have taught this single piece of information very quickly, simply by telling students. But instead she wanted them to understand what it meant and to experience it for themselves. This takes more time. It is better to teach a few topics well than many poorly. A teacher with a constructivist background will be willing to leave the curriculum if it is necessary to allow more time for students to understand. Sarah, like Julie, had also been conscientious about developing a strict lesson plan, but she was more relaxed in the classroom, and was happy to 'let the lesson plan go' and let the lesson simply roll along. Sarah's plan was more general, while Julie's specified almost what she should be doing in every minute.

As mentioned above one of the key points of constructivism is that learning is more successful in a group environment. Julie's classroom did not encourage group work. As in many conventional classrooms the students sit in rows facing the teacher, and thus cannot interact easily with other students. This fits in with the behaviorist view that learning is individual. To promote constructivist learning students should be asked to sit or work in small groups where they can easily talk and work together. Sarah tried to do this by placing herself in the middle of the class. For work that involves the whole class students should sit either in a circle or in a 'U' shape, so that everyone is 'at the front' and that everyone can participate equally.

One thing not considered in our example is assessment. Again there are big differences between traditional and constructivist classes. In a traditional class after being taught a specific topic, students are expected to demonstrate their knowledge and understanding of this topic. Students would typically answer questions from a textbook or write out a lab report. In constructivism however, assessment is interwoven throughout the entire lesson, and is not simply seen as the final activity of the lesson. There are a number of reasons for this. Firstly constructivism emphasizes the prior knowledge of the students. Before a teacher can begin the lesson they have to find out what the students already know about a topic. How and what the teacher teaches should depend on what the students already know. Teachers need to know at what stage the students are at, what misconceptions they have, and what ideas they already possess. A second reason for assessment to be interwoven throughout the lesson in constructivism is that it is also important to find out how well students are at the process skills of science. In traditional lesson how well the student's work like scientists is not important, but in constructivism it takes on more importance.

The way in which Julie and Sarah interacted with their classes was very different. Julie saw herself as the 'teacher', the ones with the knowledge, who was responsible for passing information onto the students. Sarah, however, did not really 'teach' the class anything! She started a class discussion in which they gave their own ideas. She was kinds of mediator, helping the students develop an experiment on their own, and simply used probing questions to direct them. In a constructivist classroom the student is not an 'empty vessel' into which the teacher has to pour information, students are capable of independent thought and of developing ideas for themselves. Students have to be teased and coaxed to form new ideas and ways of thinking, and that can only be done by asking them leading questions, showing them unexpected events, and by letting them work for themselves.

Meeting Science Teacher Educators

Bruce Marlowe is the co-author of Creating and Sustaining the Constructivist Classroom and is a Professor of Educational Psychology and Special Education at Roger Williams University, New England.

"Constructivism means helping students focus on: constructing knowledge, not receiving it; analyzing, not memorizing; applying, not repeating; being active, rather than passive. It means teachers need to talk less, ask more. It means students should be encouraged to ask each other questions. As Deborah Meier has said, [good] teaching is mostly listening and learning is mostly telling.

In general, to teach in a constructivist way teachers need to get out of the limelight and create conditions in the classroom that allow, encourage, foster student-driven inquiry. There are no real methods per se, although several approaches lend themselves nicely to constructivist classrooms. Establishing constructivist learning environments is extraordinarily difficult, and even more so when one learned in traditional classroom settings. A lot of unlearning is often required.

Good teachers meet their students where they are. Age is not always relevant. Indeed, often it is not relevant at all. Learning should be turned upside down, and we should think of classrooms as places where students investigate the answers to *their own questions*."

Pioneers of Constructivism and their teaching methods

Jean Piaget and the stages of cognitive development

Although the talk of children might seem like illogical nonsense to adults, Piaget discovered that children simply think in a different way to adults. Children have their own logic and rules of thought. Piaget studied how children think and developed a theoretical framework for how a child's thought processes develop. Piaget found that children pass thorough 4 different stages of cognitive development.

- *Sensorimotor* (0-2 years) in this stage children learn mostly by the use of their senses.
- *Preoperations* (3-7 years) learning is intuitive, children's motor skills develop.
- *Concrete operations* (8-11 years) Children are capable of logical thought, but are not able to use abstract thought. Children need some concrete activity to stimulate learning.
- *Formal operation* (12-15 years) During this stage children are capable of abstract thought.

The age at which individual children reach each stage can vary. Piaget's theory led to the development of learning principles for each stage. In the Sensimotor stage children need stimulating environments with many things to play with. While in the concrete operational stage children need to order, classify and locate using concrete examples.

Piaget's work shows that learners need to be involved in active activities. The activities given to children need to match the stage of cognitive development they are at. Piaget's work proved the foundation for constructivist theory and that learners build knowledge rather than receiving it.

Piaget's published a number of books with his ideas, including: *The construction of reality in the child* (1954), *Judgment and reasoning in the child* (1959), *Science of education and the Psychology of the Child (1969)*.

Lev Vygotsky and the zone of proximal development

The Belarusian Developmental Psychologist Lev Vygotska is most well known for his concept of the zone of proximal development (Vygotska 1934). This considers the importance of the social environment on the learning capabilities of an individual. When a learner or learners work without help on a task he or she is said to be at his or her actual development level. With the help of others the amount he or she learns can be increased, and this is known as the potential development level. This idea is important for the idea of 'scaffolding' of work. Vygotsky's theory shows the importance of social learning and has important implications for teaching theory. Individuals learn best in cooperative setting where others aid them.

John Dewey and 'Learning by doing'

John Dewey advocated the idea of 'learning by doing'. This was not a new idea and had been proposed numerous times in history, most notably by Confucius. In his book *'How we think'* (1933), Dewey emphasized that students should learn critical thinking and problem solving skills rather than the simple rote learning of facts. Students should be involved in hands-on tasks where they have the chance to see how things work by actually doing them for themselves. The thinking behind Dewey's ideas was that people learn best when they actually have to do something, instead of merely being told what happens. For example you cannot learn to drive a car by reading a book, the only way to learn to drive is to actually get in a car and drive around the streets.

John Dewey's ideas were of great influence in changing how people viewed education in the United States in the 20th century, but although his ideas were widely accepted by the pedagogical establishment, they failed to gain widespread use in schools. A natural extension of 'learning by doing' is the discovery learning method developed by Jerome Brunner.

Jerome Bruner and Discovery Learning

Discovery Learning is a method of learning where students are given the opportunity to explore and manipulate objects. By being allowed to do this learners generate questions and then develop possible answers to these questions. Learners are able to use discovery learning to build new ideas and knowledge. The basic tenet behind discovery learning is that learners will be more able to remember something if they have discovered it themselves, instead of merely being told it by a teacher (Bruner 1967).

Jerome Brunner was influential in defining discovery learning, but the work of Jean Piaget, and John Dewey was also important in its conception. Discovery learning is most obvious in problem solving situations. The idea of discovery learning draws on important constructivist ideas such as hands-on learning, relevance to the learner, and the fact that learning is personal.

A good example of discovery learning would be where a teacher gives students springs, pulleys, ramps and marbles and then leave the students to experiment on their own. By being allowed to handle the materials the students will discover principles of physics for themselves. The teacher would not provide any direct teaching.

The validity of discovery learning has been called into question in recent years. Many topics are simply too complex or difficult to be 'discovered', and need to be taught directly. In order to conduct science correctly students need to understand and use the science process skills: and this is not developed in discovery learning. Discovery learning is probably of most value with young children and at the beginning of an inquiry exercise where it can be used to introduce a topic.

Examples of Constructivist teaching methods

While reading the above sections some of the features of a Constructivist classroom should have become apparent. The main features of a Constructivist classroom are introduced in more detail here using examples.

'Open' or 'open ended' learning

Bernd Mosler, a teacher who specializes in open teaching techniques, taught an excellent 'open' lesson about how candles burn. He started simply be letting students observe and draw a candle flame. Then he asked students to describe how the candle burnt. One student causally remarked that the candle 'disappears' as it burns. 'Where?' asked Bernd. He then suggested experiments the students could do with their candles. For example, the hot air above a candle flame can be lighted. If you blow a candle out a stream of wax smoke is produced, and the candle can be relight simply by placing a lit split in this smoke and nowhere near the wick. Bernd offered no explanations for why these things happened, but simply questioned students to find explanations themselves. This is open learning.

When science educators talk about science lessons being 'open' or 'open ended' what they mean is that the student is not told what they are expected to find out before they begin to experiment. It can also be used to mean that the student decides the direction of the lesson and what is ultimately learnt. In an open lesson the student discovers for himself or herself what is to be learnt as the lesson progresses.

In a non-open lesson about candles the teacher might start the lesson with an explanation about how and why candles burn. The students would then have the chance to experiment with candles to confirm what they have been told. They would look for things the teacher had described or results that were expected. This is not an open lesson. However, the lesson by Bernd was open; the students were not told what they were expected to find, they had to find it themselves. Some enthusiastic students might even discover other things about how candles burn, leading to a topic the teacher had not even considered would be covered in the lesson. This is true open learning.

Lesson can be made 'open' simply by rearranging experiments. Open teaching more exactly mirrors scientific research. When scientists are conducting real research it is 'open'; they do not know what they are going to find.

'Active' learning

When I used to have problems learning new words my German teacher at school would say to me 'use it three times and its yours.' What she was trying to get across it that it is far easier to learn something if you actually use it, than if are simply told it and try to remember it.

Science is the same. You learn best when you are doing something, instead of simply being passive. Bernd could have taught his class about combustion in candles simply by getting them to write down chemical formula on the board, but instead he knew his class would really remember better if they themselves could hold a candle, see a candle, and do the experiments themselves. Active learning is simply where students get to do something. It is more than simply listening. A learner needs to be made to solve problems, answer questions, discuss and explain, to do or to make. Basically anything which forces the student to take part in the lesson in an active way.

The opposite of active learning is passive learning, this is where the learner simply is told what they need to know and must simply absorb it. A good analogy of this would be the stereotypical university lecture where the lecturer talks for an hour and the students simply listen. At the end of the hour the students have learnt nothing. There are a number of ways to promote active learning in a classroom:

- Do practical work: this engages students by allowing them to do something themselves which they must think about.
- Introduce discussion into the class. This forces students to express themselves and think about the issues involved.
- Get students to write short pieces of work during the lesson, to solve a problem or answer questions during the lesson. This makes the students actually do something.
- Get students to work together. In a cooperative setting ideas are spread and retained more easily.

The teacher as mediator: Student centered learning

In Berndt Moslers lesson about candles he did not walk into the class and start reciting all that he knew about combustion in the candle. He could have done. Instead he did the equivalent of saying, 'well, I don't know much about burning in the candle, what do you know?' He taught his lesson on the principal of 'you tell me, not me tell you.' In this way the student becomes the center of the lesson and not the teacher.

As mentioned before, traditionally teachers have been considered as sources of knowledge and their job is passing on this knowledge to their students. Common sense would make you think that therefore students with a teacher who has much subject knowledge should learn more than students with a teacher with hardly any subject knowledge. This leads to a situation where teachers feel they must 'know' everything and always be 'right'!

Because constructivism emphasizes that students must themselves construct knowledge the teacher in a constructivist classroom has a different job to do. The teacher has to provide the tools in which learners can develop understanding. It is no good the teacher simply repeating a list of facts that the students must learn, instead the teacher must provide the students with the opportunity to find and understand the facts for themselves.

For a teacher in a constructivist classroom it is more important that they are able to teach their students how and where to find the answers themselves. This means it is important teachers understand how scientific research is done. Teachers do not need to be expert biologists, chemist or physicists, but rather expert educators and expert researchers.

Inquiry-based science: Connecting science and Constructivism

While reading the last few chapters you should have become aware of the shared features of constructivist learning and of how science is conducted. They contain many shared features. For example the constructivist learning theory relies strongly on the students pre-existing ideas and own experiences, and in the same way scientists work to improve or add to the existing body of scientific knowledge which has already been produced. As nicely explained by McBride et al (2004) Newton expressed this same idea when he stated that if he had seen further than others, it was because he had been stood on the shoulder of giants.

Science today contains many of the features of constructivism, but this was not always the case. The theory of how science is conducted has changed gradually over the past century. The old view of conducting science is called 'positivism'. Scientists with a positivist viewpoint believed scientists tried to prove whether something was correct or not. Scientists, with the use of experimental techniques, believed they would be able to find a single truth. The scientist was a cold logical thinker; his conclusions were made on the basis of the results of his experiments. Personal thoughts, ideas and previous knowledge were not considered in the experimental process. Scientists based their conclusions solely on what they saw and to fit in with their observations. Scientists worked mostly alone, developing their own ideas in isolation.

Today science contains many of the features of constructivism. Now it is realized that it is impossible for scientists to conduct science without considering their prior ideas and knowledge. A scientist's work is influenced by his or her background and thoughts. It is now seen as better to acknowledge this than to try to pretend it does not make any difference. A West African scientist may have very different ideas from a European one, but it does not mean that one is better than the other. Instead of trying to 'prove' whether something is correct or not, scientists today realize it is impossible to prove anything. Scientists simply try to find explanations for the results they have. Maybe one day another scientist will show they were wrong: there is no one single truth. No one can say for definite whether something is true or not. Today science is a collaborative activity. Scientists work in research groups in which they share ideas and thoughts. Networking is of vital importance to scientists because it allows them to spread ideas and in turn receive ideas back that might help them in their own research.

Because modern science reflects the ideas of constructivism then the best way to teach science is to use these constructivist ideas. The advantage of inquiry-based science is that it enables students to learn in a constructivist way, and in doing so teachers them how scientists actually work.

Example inquiry-based science activity
How do woodlice behave?

Description

Many inquiry-based activities have been developed in which students get to study the behavior of insects (e.g. Cox-Peterson & Olson 2001). In this activity students learnt which conditions woodlice like and how woodlice behave. This activity can also be conducted with other types of invertebrate such as maggots, stick insects, worms or beetles with only slight alterations.

Materials needed

- A stock of woodlice. Obtainable in spring and summer under rocks and bricks and in damp areas of gardens.
- Petri dishes on which woodlice can be studied.
- Additional materials needed may include a lamp, paper towels, colored paper.

Procedure

1. Students were asked to work in pairs. Each pair was given a Petri dish with 2 or 3 woodlice on it. The students were asked to observe the woodlice and to note what they see. Questions like 'What features do the woodlice have?' 'What do they look like?' and 'How do they act?' were asked.

2. The students' responses were written down as a brainstorming on the blackboard so that all students could see them.

3. Next the students were asked to plan and conduct an experiment to study woodlice behavior. Suitable topics for investigation are as follows:
   a. How fast can woodlice move?
   b. Do woodlice react differently to diet coke and regular coke?
   c. Do woodlice prefer dry or damp areas?
   d. Do woodlice prefer to walk on rough or smooth surfaces?
   e. Do woodlice prefer to walk on different colored surfaces?
   Either pair was given one of these investigation questions to study.

4. The following questions were written on the board. Students were expected to answer these questions before they began their investigations. They are the typical planning questions, used to help students plan experiments independently: What is your hypothesis? What is your investigation question?

    a. How will you set up your experiment?
    b. What results will you collect? How will you collect them?
    c. How will your results help you to answer the question?
    d. How do you think the woodlice will act?

5. Once students' ideas had been checked they were allowed to conduct their investigations.

6. At the end of the experiments the students had to answer some more questions: What did your results show? What does this mean? Did this show whether your hypothesis and initial prediction was correct or not? What does this tell you about how woodlice live?

7. To extend the activity groups could be asked to produce a poster of what they did, either in class or as homework. Another good homework activity is to ask students to find out more about woodlice, using books and or the Internet to find out how they live. Students can be asked to write their findings as a written report. Students can also be asked to generate new questions that they could answer about woodlice.

SECTION:

B

WHAT DO INQUIRY-BASED SCIENCE LESSONS LOOK LIKE?

WHAT SHOULD AN INQUIRY LESSON CONTAIN?

The strongest arguments prove nothing so long as the conclusions are not verified by experience. Experimental science is the queen of sciences and the goal of all speculation.

Roger Bacon

In the first few chapters of this book we have simply placed the theoretical foundation stones of inquiry-based learning into place. We began by giving an explanation of what inquiry-based science was, and by explaining that children should learn about science by working in the same way as scientists. We then went on to describe how scientist's work and the skills they need and use when conducting research. In the last chapter we looked at the constructivist theory of learning upon which inquiry-based science is based.

Now it is time to bring all these things together and to look at how an inquiry-based lesson is structured and how it makes students work in the same way as scientists. The essential features of inquiry-based learning are given, and then how these can be integrated into an inquiry-based lesson described. In the following chapter an example of how an inquiry-based lesson about pendulums can be structured is shown.

Essential features of inquiry

The National Science Education Standards (2000) identified 5 essential features seen when students are engaged in authentic inquiry.
- Learners are engaged by scientifically orientated questions.
- Learners give priority to evidence, which allows them to develop and evaluate explanations that address scientifically orientated questions.
- Learners formulate explanations from evidence to address scientifically orientated questions.
- Learners evaluate their experiences in the light of alternative explanations, particularly those reflecting scientific understanding.
- Learners communicate and justify their proposed explanations.

The first point is quite easy to understand. In science students should be made to work with and try to answer scientific questions. Experiments should be done to answer some specific question and to solve some problem. Ideally these questions should come from the student, but in many cases they will have to be provided by the teacher. The basis for experimental work should be a single answerable investigation question.

The second point is a little more difficult to understand and elucidate, but basically refers to how students are expected to complete science experiments. Students should have the opportunity to plan and design experiments, and this should force them to think about the data they need to collect and what it will tell them. Learners need to realize that it is no good simply 'doing an experiment' and hoping the results they collect will tell them something. The experiment has to be designed to give meaningful results. Students need to understand the ideas behind variables and controls and be able to use them when designing and conducting experiments. The teacher must not simply provide 'recipe' like instructions for each experiment; students should instead plan and decide how experiments are conducted.

After designing and conducting an experiment to answer some scientific investigation question, students should then be able to consider the results they have collected and draw some conclusion or make an explanation based on them. This explanation should refer to the initial question they were trying to answer. Students should be forced to explain why they think they obtained the results they did, and why the results support the conclusions they made.

The fourth point says that once students have made an explanation based on the results they collected, they should evaluate this explanation and consider whether it fits into the evidence they already have. Students should also consider different ways of looking at the evidence, and consider if this leads to different explanations. Students should decide which explanation is the best with the data that they have. The last point is also fairly easy to understand. The students should be forced to communicate their results to others.

If these points needed to be summarized in simple words, then it would be that the student has to 1) develop a question 2) plan and conduct an experiment 3) make a conclusion 4) evaluate the conclusion 5) communicate your results. Do these points sound familiar? If you look back at chapter 2 and the steps of doing science you will see these points mirror the ones seen there and which scientists use when they do science research.

How can you structure an inquiry-based lesson?

A possible way of organizing lessons to follow the steps used by scientists is given below. This plan is based on ideas from Schwab (1962), Herron (1971) and Germann et al. (1996). If you could watch a scientist at work, hopefully you could 'tick off' each of the points in turn. The important thing to remember is that in an inquiry-based lesson the student should be the one doing the work. A scientist is not told what to do, but decides themselves what to do, likewise if the student is really to work like a scientist they have to make the decisions. The problem is not deciding how to structure inquiry-based learning, but making sure it is the student who does the research.

A possible structure for an inquiry-based science lesson

An introduction
During the introduction you aim to:
- Introduce the topic of study.
- Engage the student's interest in the topic.
- Find what knowledge the students have of the topic.
- Discover any misconceptions the students have.

Generating questions and a hypothesis
You have to get students to:
- Think of an investigation question or problem they would like to answer or solve.
- Turn this investigation question into a hypothesis that they can test.

This is widely accepted as being the most difficult thing to get students to do independently (e.g. Colburn 1997, Carin et al. 2005) Often you have to provide students with these to allow them to continue with inquiry.

Planning the experiment
Next you have to get students to plan an experiment to test their hypothesis. Student's need to:
- Identify variables.
- Think about using a control.
- Design which observations to make and which data to record.
- Design how to record data.
- Make a prediction of what might happen.

Conducting the experiment
When students conduct their experiment they should:
- Follow their plan and not be given specific instructions.
- Be able to make observations, manipulate the experimental set-up to optimize data collection, record results etc.

The important thing is that the experiment is hands-on. The students need to do it for themselves.

Concluding

Students need to be helped to do the following independently:

- Interpret results independently e.g. be able to decide what graphs, tables and results mean.
- Recognize relationships between variables.
- Be able to draw conclusions from the evidence they have collected.
- Find limitations of their experiments.

Evaluation and Communication

At the end of the exercise or lesson students should be made to:

- Communicate their results with others e.g. design a poster, give a talk, and discuss their results in class.
- Decide whether their initial hypothesis was correct or not.
- Generate new questions to investigate.
- Connect the work to their everyday lives e.g. after a practical about electricity talk about electricity in the home, or after a lesson about pollution recognize pollution in their own neighborhood.
- See the relevance of their work in other contexts e.g. they made a mini generator just like the one on your bike that powers your lights e.g. the mini-ecosystem which you made work in just the same way as your pond at home.

When designing an inquiry lesson you could try to follow the structure shown here. Look at the points given here and try to use them. The more of these skills your students use the more inquiry-like will your lesson be. Now we have gone through these points, we will look at how some of them can be integrated into a science experiment in the next chapter.

Meeting Inquiry Teachers

Dr. Norman Budnitz taught middle and high school science and mathematics for 22 years at Carolina Friends School, Durham, NC. In 1997, he co-founded the Center for Inquiry-Based Learning (CIBL) at Duke University with Professor Stephen A. Wainwright. CIBL is dedicated to improving science education in K-8 classrooms by helping teachers understand and use inquiry-teaching methods.

Author: What should inquiry-based lessons contain for them to be inquiry?
NB: Students should have the opportunity to explore something interesting, ask a question or two about it, and then try to find out the answer to their questions. This will probably lead to even more questions. The teacher should be a guide in this exploration, not just a fount of knowledge. Since an inquiry lesson can take many forms, there is no one answer to this question. I think there is no single factor that makes a lesson inquiry-based. Inquiry is too many things.

Author: What should students be doing in an inquiry-based lesson?
NB: Students should be playing the role of scientists: observing, asking questions, trying to find answers.

How does an inquiry-based lesson differ from a 'normal' or 'traditional' lesson?
NB: Students are active in the learning process. They have to think, reason, and problem-solve. They are not just empty vessels to be filled up with facts and vocabulary handed out by teachers and textbooks. In other words, there's more to learning science than just memorizing. The inquiry process requires real 'seeing,' not just looking, real 'thinking,' not just memorizing.

Author: How is an inquiry-based lesson analogous to real science?
NB: That depends on the level of inquiry in the lesson. Some topics can be presented as recipes, but the students are asked to design their own data sheets rather than fill out a work sheet designed by the teacher. In a more intense version of inquiry, the students ARE being scientists. There's really no difference from real science, except perhaps for the level of thoroughness expected or required.

AN EXAMPLE OF AN INQUIRY-BASED SCIENCE LESSON

We can lick gravity, but sometimes the paperwork is overwhelming.

Wernher von Braun

What affects how a pendulum swings?

This chapter provides an outline for an inquiry-based science lesson about pendulums. Students get to conduct experiments to study the factors that affect how a pendulum swings. This exercise is a very commonly used example of how physics can be taught using inquiry-based science. It has a number of advantages including its simpleness, cheapness and the fact that many students will possess misconceptions over what affects the rate pendulums swing at. Various versions of this experiment can be found, one example of an inquiry-based lesson using this theme has been written by Donaldson & Odom (2001). This is our version.

Lesson aims

- Students studied the factors that affect the rate at which a pendulum swings.
- Students practiced designing and conducting experiments.

Introduction

The first thing we needed to do was to introduce the idea of a pendulum to the students. We wanted to do this in an interesting way that would hopefully engage the students and make them interested in the lesson they were going to have. We also wanted to find out what the children already knew about pendulums and how they swing.

The best way of doing these things that we could think of was to make a large pendulum in the middle of the classroom where everyone could see it. Using a hook that was already in the ceiling we suspended a long piece of thick string, about 2.5 meters in length, and then on its end we fastened a large ball of play dough. This made a very large pendulum that the students simply could not ignore! It could be swung around the class, and reached most of the students. Because the pendulum was suspended in the middle of the classroom all the students were sat around the pendulum and no one was 'at the back.'

At this stage we did not explain what we were doing or question the students in any way. They simply observed us as we put the pendulum together. When we began to swing the pendulum the students became instantly attentive! They had to duck out of the way of the pendulum, or move their chairs to allow it to swing freely. (Note: we did not push the pendulum with much force, and cautioned the students from making the pendulum swing too quickly. A fast moving ball of play dough can hurt if it hits you, especially if it is unexpected).

We asked students to take turns swinging the pendulum, and in this way ensured that many students became involved in the lesson right from the beginning. Sometimes we simply asked students to let the pendulum swing until it lost momentum, while at other times we prompted students to stop the pendulum in mid-swing and to re release it.

As the students were swinging the pendulum we began to ask them questions about what they were seeing and doing. What makes the pendulum swing? What would happen if you changed the length of the pendulum? How many swings does the pendulum make in a minute? How does the pendulum move? Does it follow the same sized arc every time? Why not? How long does it swing for before stopping?

We continued with the large pendulum for 15 minutes before dismantling it again, and then moving onto the next stage of the lesson. The students had had many good ideas, and now we wanted to record them before they were forgotten. We began a simple brainstorming exercise on the blackboard. We recorded some of the ideas the students had already had and with further questioning got some more ideas. The brainstorming below is not the same as the one we made that day, but is just an example to give you an idea of what a brainstorming about pendulums might look like.

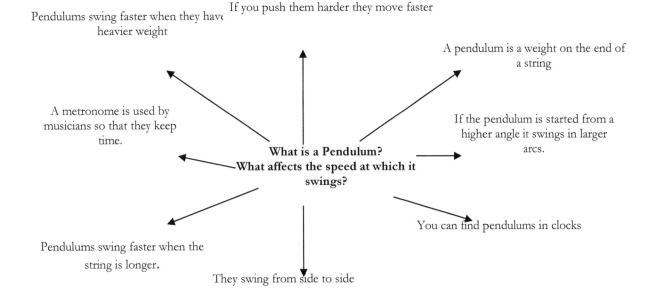

Pendulums swing faster when they have heavier weight

If you push them harder they move faster

A pendulum is a weight on the end of a string

A metronome is used by musicians so that they keep time.

If the pendulum is started from a higher angle it swings in larger arcs.

What is a Pendulum? What affects the speed at which it swings?

Pendulums swing faster when the string is longer.

You can find pendulums in clocks

They swing from side to side

If you did not want to build a large pendulum in the class because of time constraints, you could instead bring a pendulum clock to the class and then ask your students to observe and answer questions about it. However, the main
disadvantage of this is that the students are not as involved as when they could actually touch and see a pendulum moving around the classroom.

Generating an investigation question and a hypothesis

Now we had successfully introduced the topic we wanted students to move onto the first stage of a scientific investigation, namely the thinking of a good investigation question and then the making of a hypothesis. Because of the activities the students had already done this was relatively easy, all the information the students needed was already in place and ready to be used.

First we asked students to recap on the factors they thought affected the rate at which a pendulum swings. The students offered a number of ideas. As the students commented on the following few ideas we listed them in the blackboard. However, no comment was criticized. The three variables that could affect the rate of swinging which we wrote down were:

- The length of the string.
- The angle at which the pendulum is first swung from.
- The mass of the weight at the end of the pendulum.

These three points provided the basis for the experiments for the rest of the session. We divided the class up into groups. Each group was given one of the three variables to investigate. To help them get started each student was given an experiment prompt sheet. The experiment sheets contained questions that prompted students to think about different aspects of their experiments. The experiment prompt sheet was split into three different parts, one part was designed to help students develop a question and hypothesis, another was to help students plan, and lastly there was a conclusion section with questions prompting students to make conclusions.

Obviously how the students complete the sentences to do with finding an investigation question and hypothesis depended on which group they were in. We circulated around the class offering help where it was required, but we were surprised at the ease students had at developing a suitable question and hypothesis. These are the most difficult skills in inquiry-based lessons for students to master, but maybe the subject had been introduced well enough that students were capable of doing this on their own and without much help.

Planning the experiment

It is one thing deciding what to study, but it is another actually deciding how to test a hypothesis you have made. The students were now tasked with designing and planning a way of testing their hypothesis. This was done with the use of the planning questions on the experiment sheet.

What is important in this experiment is getting the students to consider the different variables involved. They need to grasp that they need to keep all the other variables the same apart from the one they are investigating themselves. The planning questions on the experimental sheet were designed to get the students to determine which were the independent, dependant and fixed variables.

It is important to emphasize that in inquiry-based science it is the student who decides how to set up the experiment, which measurements to take, and which results to write down. The students have to decide how long they want the pendulum to be, or how much weight they want there to be on its end. The students have to decide themselves whether they count how many times the pendulum swings in 1 minute, or in 2 minutes, or 5 minutes or even if they want to count how long it takes a pendulum to swing a certain number of times.

We found that often students felt 'lost' and kept asking how to set up the experiment. They felt unsure about what lengths of string to use, or what weights to use, although this is actually of little importance in the actual functioning of the experiment. Students can use string lengths of 20, 40, or 60 cm, or 10, 20, and 30 cm; it really does not matter. This is often the case with students not used to inquiry; they are unsure of themselves. What is important is that you help student's focus on what is important in the experiment, that all but one variable stays the same. If students use unsuitable lengths or weights, this can always be ironed out later through trial and error. As long as the basic idea behind the experiment is sound then alterations like this can be easily made. We circulated freely around the class listening to the discussions going on and guiding students to experimental designs that were workable.

Doing the experiment

Once the students had had their experimental plans checked by us they were allowed to go on to actually conducting the experiment. Students were provided with play dough, measuring scales in order to weigh play dough, balls of string, and timers. Students could make their pendulums however they liked, but we suggested they suspend them from their desks. It provided a spur to those groups who were still at the planning stage to finish when they saw that other groups were moving onto doing the experiments.

Through practice the students found that good lengths of string to use were 40, 60, 80 and 100 cm. Good weights to use were 25, 50, 75 and 100 grams. However, don't forget if students want to use different amounts this is also no problem.

A quiet classroom it was not! However, there is a difference between the noise students make when they are working and the noise they make when they are being rowdy. Here students were working together in their groups and the noise came from their discussions, ideas and comments as they were investigating. We simply watched and listened, and where appropriate offered advice or possible modifications. We kept an eye of each group to make sure that they were progressing. Normally a certain sign of a group that is 'lost' is when they are not talking to each other but simply 'going through the motions.'

Concluding

It is important to set a time limit for the experiments so that students have a target to work towards and that you have a certain fixed time at which you can bring the practical side of the lesson to a close. Some of our groups had already completed their experiments and had moved onto making conclusions when we instructed the rest to cease experimentation. Now we had to help the students make sense of what they had seen and the results they had collected. They had to move from making statements they simply thought were correct, to making statements that were backed up by the experiments they had done and the data they had collected.

Once again we fell back to using to using questions on the experimental sheet to prompt students to think about their conclusions. The answers the students gave to these questions provided the basis for a short discussion we started about the experiments. We selected students and asked then what had happened in their experiments? What had you found? What happened when you increased string length, or used different sized weights? What happened when the angle at which the pendulum was released was changed? What did their results say?

Pendulum Experiment Sheet

Name: Date:

Finding a Question and Hypothesis to investigate

We are studying how.........................affects how a pendulum swings.

Our question is………………………………………………….

Our hypothesis is that when we…………………the pendulum will

swing………………

Planning Questions

How will we set up our experiment?

Which things do we have to keep the same?

Which thing do we alter?

What will we record and how will we record it?

Concluding Questions

What results did you collect?

What do your results tell you?

Evaluation and communication

It is important for students to be made to evaluate the experiments they have done to think about limitations with the experiments or how they could be improved. We asked students what problems they came across, and how they thought the experiment could be made better. How could they improve the experiment? Students responded saying they needed more time, a common request, but others commented that they could have repeated the tests more to obtain more accurate results, or could have used standard weights instead of measuring out amounts of play dough.

Although we did not have time one particularly good way to get students to communicate the results they have collected is to get them to make a poster. If students make a poster after conducting an experiment it should contain information about what they did and what results they found. They could also include diagrams, pictures and drawings.

Classic inquiry-based activities

Which brand of antacid tablet is best at settling an upset stomach?

Description

In this activity students conducted an investigation to find out which brand of antacid tablet was the most effective at settling an upset stomach.

Materials
- Several brands of Antacid tablets.
- HCL of different strengths.
- pH paper or a pH meter.

Procedure

1. We introduced the lesson by demonstrating to students what happened when antacid tablets are placed in water. They quickly started to dissolve with much bubbling and hissing. We prompted the class to observe this and to think about why we take antacid tablets with questions like: What happens to the antacid tablet? What does the stomach contain? Why do you have an upset stomach? How do antacid tablets help sooth an upset stomach?

2. We asked students to work in pairs to design an investigation to find out which brand of antacid tablet is the best at settling an upset stomach. We prompted them to answer the following questions: What is your question? What is your hypothesis? How will you design your experiment? What will you measure and record? What will you use to take these recordings? Which brand do you think will be the best, why?

3. When we had checked the student's ideas for how they could conduct an experiment we allowed them to go ahead and conduct the experiment. CAUTION: If you use the same experiment ensure the students follow safety precautions and work in a safe way!

4. After all the groups had finished their experiments and had gained sufficient results we helped the students to interpret and make conclusions about their data. We asked them questions like: How could you present your results so that they are easy to interpret? What do your results show? Which brand is therefore the best?

5. Like in the example with the pendulum exercise you could ask the groups to produce a poster of their work showing the question and hypothesis they had, their method, their results, and what they mean. You could ask the student to include a section on how they could make the experiment better, or to think of other experiments they could conduct using the antacid tablets.

A number of other different inquiry-based experiments can be conducted using antacid tablets. For example, how long it takes an antacid tablet to dissolve in water can be timed; students can conduct an experiment to find if tablets dissolve quicker in warmer rather than colder water. Likewise, students can conduct an investigation to see if antacid tablet broken down into different sized lumps dissolve at different rates.

SECTION:

HOW TO DESIGN AND TEACH INQUIRY-BASED
SCIENCE LESSONS

DESIGNING AN INQUIRY-BASED SCIENCE LESSON

I love fools' experiments. I am always making them.

Charles Darwin

In the previous chapter I showed you an example of an inquiry-based lesson to help you see what inquiry involves and what it is made up of. Hopefully this has given you some ideas about how you could teach the different sections of inquiry yourself. In this chapter we will look at further methods suitable for use in an inquiry setting and elaborate on some of the methods used in the previous chapter. Hopefully once you have a good knowledge of the different methods open to you, you can start to design inquiry-based lessons of your own by choosing the methods most suitable for the lesson you want to teach.

Choosing a topic or experiment for inquiry-based science

It is important to realize that not all topics are suitable for teaching in an inquiry-based way. If you want to teach using inquiry-based science you should choose the topic you wish to teach with care. If you have a specific experiment you wish to teach using inquiry you should consider carefully if and how it can be made suitable for teaching using inquiry.

Inquiry-based teaching is best at teaching concrete rather than theoretical concepts (Colburn 2000). It is difficult to teach theoretical or abstract ideas using inquiry-based science because many students may not have reached the formal operations stage of cognitive development. It is better to choose ideas that are observable or concrete. For example inquiry is suitable for teaching students that reaction rates are dependant on the concentration of reactants, but not for teaching students about kinetic-molecular theory.

Try to center inquiry-based lessons on good investigation questions that the students will be able to answer by designing and conducting their own investigation. Inquiry-based activities are more likely to be successful if they use materials and situations that your students are comfortable with and have experience of using. Choose an activity that you feel most of the students possess the ability to succeed at.

The introduction

The actual process of inquiry begins first when the students begin to find and develop a suitable problem and question to investigate. However, it is good to start first with an introduction as this allows you to give the lesson a good constructivist setting and to engage students interest in the topic to be studied. Choose introductory activities that are interesting and fun. If children become interested at the beginning it will be much easier to hold their interest through the lesson.

There are a number of different ways in which to begin an inquiry-based science lesson. Some of these ideas are summarized below. Different methods of introducing the lesson are suitable for different topics and experiments. Consider carefully which method you believe is the best for your teaching style, the class you intend to teach, and the topic you wish to teach. Simple exploration might be most suitable for younger students, while brainstorming is probably better for older students.

Simple exploration
Maybe the best and simplest way of starting an inquiry-based lesson is to let students explore some object or process. In effect students simply get to 'mess about', 'play' or 'explore' something without direction from the teacher. Doing this allows students to gain concrete experience of something from which questions can later be asked. This is similar to the 'discovery learning' proposed by John Dewey. For this type of simple exploration to be most effective it should be short, only about 5 to 10 minutes in length.

A group of student teachers tasked with designing an inquiry-based lesson about touch developed an excellent example of simple exploration with which to begin a lesson. They developed a series of mystery boxes. These were sealed cardboard boxes with a hole on the side where you could put your hand, each mystery box contained a different object and at the start of the lesson the children had to guess what each box contained. This proved to be an excellent way to get the pupils interest.

At the end of exploration it is best if you ask the students what they have found out, and use this as the starting point for the lesson. It is important that you connect this stage with the ones that follow and not simply leave it isolated. This method is one of the most effective at stimulating interest in the students and getting them connected with the theme of the lesson.

A phenomenon activity
Another good way to introduce a topic that you could consider using is to use a phenomenon activity, discrepant event, or hook, as it is sometimes known as. This is a short and simple activity, experiment, object or model that you demonstrate to the class at the beginning of the lesson which is designed to be interesting and to grab the students attention. A phenomenon activity should make students think: 'what happened there? I did not expect that!'

One rather extreme 'phenomenon' used by Jearl Walker, a columnist for Scientific American, was when he would walk over hot coals to demonstrate firewalking through the Leidenfrost effect to chemistry classes (Levy 2000). The Leidenfrost effect is where the feet sweat so much from fear that it provides protection for the feet as the owner of the feet walks over hot coals. However you do not necessarily have to risk personal injury to provide a good phenomenon activity. Another good example of a phenomenon activity is to put an electrical current through pickles and other types of vegetable to make them glow. This would be an excellent way to introduce a lesson about electrical circuits!

One teacher who we saw teaching a lesson about sound in an inquiry-based lesson way started the lesson by making sound 'visible.' He used a small drum and by connecting it to a small bucket of water he developed a piece of equipment where circular waves were formed on the surface of the water when the drum was hit, much to the amazement of the class he was teaching. One of our student teachers wanting to teach an inquiry-based lesson about human behavior started the lesson by entering the classroom and acting like a gorilla, which caused much puzzlement and entertainment to the students involved.

There are various websites that offer different phenomenon activities. Chemistry offers the most interesting selection, with there being various ways of making bangs, smoke, and small explosions. However, they can also be much more mundane, the important thing is that you do something unexpected. The aim is only to force the students to think about the theme being studied and provide a starting point for the teacher to ask questions

Brainstorming

Brainstorming was developed by the American businessman Alan Osborn to help creative thinking (Osborn, 1952). During brainstorming sessions a problem or topic is identified, and then ideas about that problem are generated. These ideas help to suggest possible solutions to the problem, or open up new avenues for investigation. It is a way of making people look at something in a new way. Brainstorming can be a highly effective method of opening students' minds, discovering what students already know about a particular area and prompting further ideas.

When brainstorming, choose a single word or phrase connected to the problem. Place this at the center of the page, sheet or board. Then as ideas are generated about that word place them around it in an ever-increasing circle. For example, when you think about food what comes into your mind? Dinnertime, shops, recipes, flour, farmers, packaging, starvation… Words that are connected or lead from other words can be joined together. At the end of the session the brainstorming should look spidery, with numerous branches coming from the main word.

Brainstorming can be done either alone, but is most commonly used in group situations. The important thing to remember about brainstorming is that it is open, free and without criticism. Anyone should feel able to participate, even if the ideas could be seen as silly or irrelevant. Only evaluate the work after the brainstorming session has finished.

If you show students an object, picture or phenomenon, then you can then use this as the basis for brainstorming. You can ask individual students to create their own brainstorming diagrams from what they have just seen. Later, at the end of the experiment or lesson you can either ask students to draw a new brainstorming about the topic covered or ask students to change their original brainstorming diagrams to incorporate any new ideas they might have learnt. In either case, brainstorming offers a good way for you to see what students have learnt in the lesson.

Brainstorming works best when it is fast, unorganized and as broad in scope as possible. Weird, strange or unusual answers should be encouraged. Although an idea might seem irrelevant, it could in fact help open up new areas of thought. If brainstorming is done quickly people are more spontaneous and more likely to say the first thing that comes into their minds.

To use brainstorming well ensure that you do the following:

- Define the problem well at the beginning.

- No distractions. The session should remain focused on the brainstorming. It is better short and intense, than long and drawn out.

- No ideas should be criticized during the brainstorming.

- Don't follow any one idea for to long.

- Try to make it fun. It is better if everyone feels they can take part and that it is not a too serious exercise.

Brainstorming is an ideal tool to use in inquiry-based situations. It can be used at the beginning of an inquiry-based lesson to help you judge the students prior knowledge of a particular topic, and so that you can then tailor the lesson to the students needs. Brainstorming can also be used later in the lesson to help students generate ideas and questions that they can then investigate. Brainstorming is ideal for generating a list of questions that can then be narrowed down to a single good question at the end of the brainstorming that the students then design an experiment to answer.

Example Inquiry-based Science lesson

Dancing raisins!

Description

When raisins are placed in carbonated water they initially sink because they are denser than the water. After a few minutes, however, air bubbles attach to the raisins and they rise to the surface. Once at the surface the bubbles break and the raisin once again sinks.

This is a traditional discrepant event used to introduce buoyancy and density, but which Huber and Moore (2001) adapted into an interesting inquiry-based activity. In the traditional activity students would simply be asked to count how many times the raisins rose and sank. Huber and Moore's inquiry-based activity takes the lesson much further and allows students to develop their own investigations to help them understand the principles behind buoyancy and density.

Materials needed
- Raisins
- Carbonated water, ones that are clear such as sprite or lemonade are best as the raisins can be easily observed.

Procedure

1. Huber and Moore first allowed students to discover that the raisins dance. They asked students to work in pairs. Each pair was given some freshly opened carbonated water in a glass and some raisins. They were asked what they thought would happen when raisins were placed in the glass? Next they were asked to see if their predictions were correct. They were instructed to place some raisins in the carbonated water. After a few minutes the raisins began to 'dance,' and began slowly rising and falling in the carbonated water.

2. Next students were asked to think of a way to make the raisins dance faster? Examples of possible solutions to this problem include the idea that squashed raisins may travel quicker, or that raisons travel quicker in hotter or colder water.

3. The teacher gave each pair of students a variable that could affect the rate of raisin dancing and ask them to investigate whether it really did have an effect on raisin dancing or not. Students planned their investigations by providing answers to the following statements;
    a. We are going to investigate this question.
    b. We predict these findings.
    c. To answer this question, we will do these things.
    d. During our investigation we will record the following.

4. Each pair then conducted their investigation. The pairs may need to repeat the original activity to find out what speed the raisins were traveling at in the original condition. Throughout the planning and conducting stage the teacher should prompt students with appropriate discussion and questioning.

5. The students were encouraged to interpret and present their results. Did any one variable significantly affect the speed of the dancing raisins? Are the results consistent or highly variable?

At the end of the lesson the investigations were reviewed. Students were asked if they would do anything differently if they had to do the investigations again, and what other factors they now believed affected the rate of raisin dancing.

Providing pictures, objects or video clips

You can also introduce an inquiry-based lesson by using simple pictures, objects and video clips. You can use a combination of these things, and don't have to feel restricted to simply using one. For example in an inquiry-based lesson about dirty water, we first showed an article from a magazine to the students with an advert for spring fresh mountain water. Secondly we gave students a short video clip of an advert for spring water, which explained how the water was purified as it filtered through mountain rock. And lastly we showed students a real example of a water filter and how it could make dirty water clean as it was filtered. Students then had to design and make their own water filters.

The advantage of using these methods is that they are relatively easy and quick to use in the classroom. The lesson can be quickly introduced and then you can get on with teaching the lesson. This is especially important where time is limited. With phenomenon activities there is always the danger that they won't work, but when simply showing pictures or objects that risk is eliminated. You also don't need to spend long searching for suitable material if you are simply looking for a picture or an object.

<u>Ask students to list what they know</u>

A final method of introducing a topic is for you to simply ask the students what they know about it. Ask them to list their ideas in pairs or small groups. The ideas are then communicated with the class and listed on the board. Although this method allows teachers to find out what students already know about a topic it is not the most interesting way of starting a lesson. One advantage though is that it can often be easier to turn these ideas into investigation questions. It is also relatively quick, and as a time pressed teacher with only a limited amount of teaching time you might feel this is the most suitable method to use when you simply want to hurry to getting an investigation done.

Generating investigation questions and a hypothesis

<u>Generating an investigation question:</u>

It cannot be overemphasized how important it is to find and develop a good question to investigate for inquiry-based science to function properly. As should have become clear if you read the chapter about Scientific Inquiry a good starting question is the basis of all scientific investigation, and exactly the same is true of inquiry-based science. Without a good starting question your students will not be able to design and conduct an experiment, and their attempt at inquiry-based science will fail.

Unfortunately the questions children ask are not normally suitable for investigation. Children tend to ask 'Why', 'How' or 'What' questions. Why is the sky blue? How do cars work? What do cows eat? These are knowledge-based questions and the child asks them to get a specific piece of information, or simply to express an interest in something. Questions such as these cannot be used to design profitable investigations.

It should not be surprising that children pose so few questions suitable for investigation. After all most of the questions which teachers ask tend also to be knowledge based. Most teachers ask questions in order to 'test' students, to see if they know something or to see if they have remembered something.

The first thing you need to do is to make sure that you yourself understand what exactly a good investigation question is. This is especially important for teachers without a science background who may not know how to start a scientific investigation and may not be sure of which questions are needed.

An investigation question is a question that can be answered by conducting an experiment. Investigation questions should aim to answer a single specific solvable problem. For example 'How do plants grow?' is not a good investigation question, it is too broad and it is unclear what exactly needs to be studied. Can you think of an experiment to find out how plants grow? However, the question 'What effect does temperature have on plant growth?' is a much better investigation question. It is clear what you want to find out. It would not be too difficult to design an experiment to answer this question. Here are some examples of questions that are too broad and not suitable:

'What are trees like?'

'How does the heart work?'
'Why do we breathe?'
'How do stick insects behave?'
'How do mice behave?'
'What is density?'

Can you design an experiment to answer these questions? If not, then neither can your students. These questions may be good as the title of a topic area but cannot be used in an experiment easily. Consider these questions instead:

'Do different trees have different heights?'
'What things make your heart beat faster?'
'How fast do stick insects move?'
'Which foods are mice able to smell along a maze?'
'What shape of objects sink or swim?'

Would you be able to design an experiment to answer these questions? These questions are much more specific and can be used in an experimental setting. These are the questions you should aim to get students to generate during an inquiry-based lesson.

Now you understand what exactly an investigation question is you have to find ways to get your students to make them. This is probably the most difficult stage of the inquiry-process and the one which students will have most difficulty with. Often you will have to provide a question that the students can use because they will not be able to create one on their own. This does not mean the lesson is no longer inquiry-based, only that it is at a lower level of inquiry than it would be if the students developed their own question to investigate.

You need to try to train students to ask good questions. Maybe the best way of doing this is to use and pose investigation questions yourself and to use investigation questions around the classroom. For example you could include investigation questions on wall displays or around science areas. You can ask students to occasionally make their own questions about a topic they have answered questions on for homework or after they have read part of a book. If students are gradually introduced to these types of questions they will find it much easier to ask suitable questions later on.

Generation of a hypothesis:
A hypothesis is a single statement that scientists make about the problem they are studying. An experiment is then done to see if the hypothesis is correct or not. An experiment is really a kind of hypothesis testing. There is some disagreement over the importance of getting students to develop a hypothesis to be tested. The reason for this is that often scientists often do not develop a hypothesis until later in their investigations. However, what is important is to get the students to predict what could happen. Even if the students are not asked to develop a hypothesis they should be made to guess what might happen in the experiment.

The most frequently used method to get students to develop a hypothesis is the 'if…then…' statement. **If** one thing is altered **then** this should happen. Getting students to form a hypothesis should be relatively straightforward compared with getting them to generate a suitable question to investigate.

Providing investigation questions

Even if you have to provide students with the investigation question you can still do so in a way that helps them learn how to form them. Maybe sometime in the future they will 'catch on' and not need your help. A good way of doing this is to take suitable points from a brainstorming, list them, and then provide the investigation question beside them. For example:

What factors influence how a plant grows? (the original question given to students to answer)

Student generated words	Teacher generated investigation question
Heat	Do plants in warmer places grow quicker?
Water	Do plants given more water grow faster than plants given less water?
Light	Do plants grown in lighter places grow faster than plants in darker places?

The students can then take the investigation questions you have generated and continue their investigations. You could form the first investigation question from the first word for the students, and then ask your students to turn the remaining words into suitable investigation questions.

Practice at reforming questions for experiments

To help students practice making suitable investigation questions you can give them unsuitable questions and then ask them to turn them into questions that are suitable for investigation. For example:

Initial Question:
Why do we wear clothes?

Question suitable for investigation:
Does insulation slow the rate at which water cools?

Using hypothesis cards

This method also gives students practice in deciding and evaluating. You can write down a number of hypotheses on cards that refer to a specific topic and then ask the students to decide which ones are most suitable to investigate. You could get students to rank what they think is most suitable.

Initial Question:
Why does my plant grow towards the window?

Possible Hypothesizes:
Plants grow towards the light because:

- The plant likes glass products.
- The plant is attracted to the radiator.
- Plants are allergic to people so grow away from where they live.
- Plants naturally bend one way or another.
- The plant is too big and has naturally fallen down one way.

Planning the experiment

Planning is an important stage of the experimental process, but one which teachers often neglect (Harlen 1985). Students need to consider and think about what they intend to do and how they intend to do it. The planning of experiments is a problem-solving skill, in which students have to work out how to tackle some problem to find some answer. Although experiments should be planned, you should realize that plans change as the students begin experimenting. Students' ideas may change when they actually have to do the investigation and they are faced with problems or ideas they did not think about or realize before they began actually experiencing the practical at first hand.

Students should aim to produce a 'fair test'; one which can be reasonably be said to be accurate and which shows in some conclusive way the effect of one thing on another. When planning an experiment students typically have to work out which variables are present, which variable needs to be changed in the experiment (the independent variable), which variables should be kept the same (fixed or controlled variables), and which variable should be observed for a change (dependant variable). Students also need to consider what they will record and how they will record it.

The easiest way in which to get students to plan and think about an experiment is simply just to ask them what they intend to do. As part of a class discussion you can pose questions to the students that force them to identify the variables in the experiment that they want to change and the ones they want to keep the same. What do you want to find out? What things can change? Which of these do you want to study? How will you find out if this has an effect on that? What will you keep the same?

You could also prompt students to think about what results they want to collect and how they want to collect them and the reasons for these choices. What will you measure? Why? How will you measure it? Other ways of helping students are given below, but should all be used in conjunction with good questioning from the teacher. You need to probe students' answers to make sure they have thought fully about what they are going to do, and that they understand how the experiment will work. If you make planning and experimental design a distinct step in the experimental process students will come to appreciate its importance.

Finding the correct sequence or filling in gaps

To practice their skills at developing methods, you could give the steps contained in a scientific method in the incorrect order, and then have your students attempt to place them in the correct order again. Another similar idea you can use is to remove key words from the method and to let the students guess what they could be. This method gets students to think about why they are doing something. For example in the following text, students might not know the answers, but can come up with guesses as to what they are. You can prompt them with questions. What does food contain?

A method for finding whether food contains …

Collect together several different types of foodstuff, for example…, … and… Cut the food into thin slices. Place … drops of … onto the food. Observe which color it turns. If the food turns a … color this shows that … is present.

Planning sheets

A commonly suggested method of helping students plan is to use a planning sheet (e.g. Preddy 2006, Sang & Wood-Robinson 2002) A planning sheet prompts students to think about the experiment they will do and think about the factors they need to consider in the experiment. A planning sheet is not a 'worksheet'. A worksheet might ask the students the answers to questions that require knowledge. A planning sheet on the other hand gets students to think and requires little prior knowledge about the topic being learnt. A planning sheet is a good method to get students on the way to full open inquiry.

A planning prompt sheet

In today's science lesson the topic I learned about was…………………………………

The aspect that I am going to investigate is……………………………………………..

The question that I want to ask is………………………………………………………..

The variables that affect this question are………………………………………………..

The variable I want to change is…………………………………………………….

The variable I will study is…………………………………………………………..

I will keep these variables the same…………………………………………………….

What I am going to do is……………………………………………………………..

The apparatus I will use is……………………………………………………………..

My test will be fair and give scientific results because……………………………..

What I expect to find out is……………………………………………………………..

I think this will happen because………………………………………………………..

<u>A Planning Board</u>
Another good suggestion to help students plan experiments is to use a planning board (Sang & Wood-Robinson 2002). A planning board can be completed either individually or in small groups, but is perhaps most suitable for use with the class as a whole as part of a teacher led class discussion. The idea is that students think of ideas for the gaps. These ideas can be written on 'post-it' notes and then stuck into the correct place or if the board is used simply written into the gap. If new or better ideas are generated or ideas change during the discussion then it is possible to remove or wipe away an idea and replace it with a new one.

<u>Suggested materials table</u>
Another way in which you can help students decide how to conduct an experiment is to provide them with a range of equipment. This can helps prompt students think of ideas for their experiments. You could provide a selection of lab equipment on a table and allow the students to see what they could use. Alternatively you could write a list of the available equipment on the board.

'Double dipping'

A good example of a way to get students to practice planning and designing experiments was provided by Favero (1998). In one lesson he gives students the problem of 'double dipping' to think about. Double dipping is where an individual dips a chip into ketchup, mayonnaise or another kind of dip, bites an end off, and then redips the chip. Double dipping is considered antisocial as it may spread germs from the eaters' mouth on the half eaten chip to the communal pot of mayonnaise. Favero gives his students the double dipping scenario and then asks them how they would design an experiment to find out if double dipping really did pass germs from the half eaten chip to the mayonnaise. This is conducted purely as a paper exercise and is not carried out as an experiment. Students came up with a variety of experimental ideas to solve this problem, including analyzing the mayonnaise for bacteria after it has been double dipped, using dyes to represent saliva or germs and seeing if they contaminate the mayonnaise from half eaten chips, and the rather dubious idea of getting someone with a cold to double dip then seeing if people who use the dip afterwards catch a cold. The exercise is good example of getting students to think up and design experimental procedures, an important part of the inquiry process.

An example of a planning board:

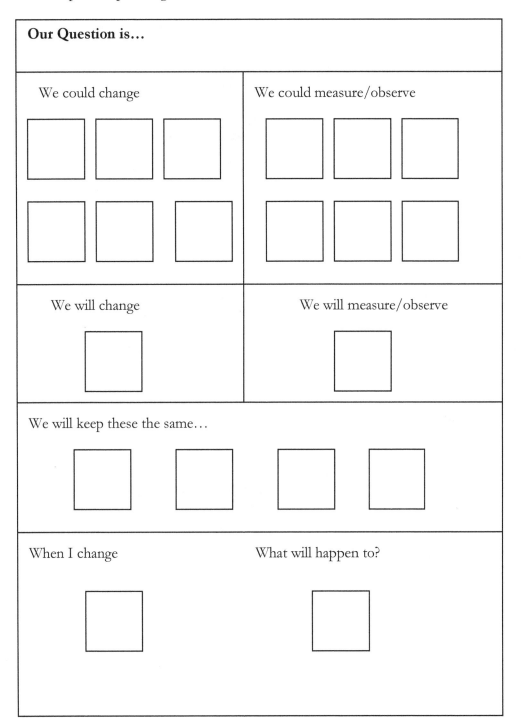

Our Question is...

We could change

We could measure/observe

We will change

We will measure/observe

We will keep these the same...

When I change

What will happen to?

Conducting the experiment

During this stage of the inquiry-based lesson students get the chance to put their plans into action. You might think that you might have little to do during this stage of the inquiry lesson. After all the students have planned and designed their experiments and presumably know what they have to do, so surely you can sit down and take a break? Unfortunately not. There is still plenty for a teacher to do during this stage. It is best if you constantly move around the class while groups are experimenting. This means you can keep an eye on what is happening and are available if support is needed. You should observe closely what is happening in each group and be ready to ask questions to make sure everyone is heading in the correct direction. You have to try to find the right balance between meddling and being passive. You don't want to interrupt students if they are in full flow, but you also don't want to sit back and do nothing if groups are obviously floundering.

Interpretation of results

This stage corresponds to the 'conclusion' of many experiments. During this stage students need to look at and interpret the results they have collected. Students need to be able to spot patterns and see relationships in the results. The students must make a conclusion or an explanation for the results they have. In other word, during this stage, the students have to make sense of the information they have collected and realize what it tells them.

This is another important stage of the experimental process which teachers often neglect. In non-inquiry lessons this stage often seems to become detached from the rest of the experimental process; the students conduct an experiment, after which the teacher gives them a short abstract conclusion which does not make the connection between the work the students did and the results they collected and the conclusion reached. "In conclusion plant growth increases as temperature rises." In an inquiry-based lesson the teacher must make sure that 'concluding' is not just a single sentence summing up, but that it is connected with the experiment done, and that it is a carefully thought out process, leading to ideas which can be justified.

<u>Concluding prompt sheets</u>
Concluding prompt sheets are similar to the prompt sheets used in the planning stage, but instead they ask students to think about their results (Preddy 2006, Sang & Wood-Robinson 2002).

Concluding prompt sheet 1

Looking at my results I noticed that as…………then…………………

This was expected/not expected because……………………………….

The reason for this pattern is……………………………………………

So my conclusion …………………………………………………………

Concluding prompt sheet 2

I have been investigating……………………………………………………

The results table headings are……………………………………………

Plotting a graph of……………………against……………………………

The graph will show a connection between………....and………………

The shape of my graph is…………………….., which shows me that as

…………………so………………………………………………………

My conclusion is………………………………………………………..

My explanation for this is…………………………………………….

75

Evaluation

An important feature of science research is the communication of information. Although many people believe scientists are some lonely breed who sit all day in their labs this is simply not true! The scientist who sits in a lab all day doing research, not talking to anyone or showing anyone his work is a failure. To be a successful scientist you have to show the world what you are doing. There are a number of ways an aspiring scientist can do this. There are a large number of science journals in which scientists publish results of experiments they have done. Scientists also visit conferences at which they can give talks and present posters. Scientists talk about what they do with their work partners and colleagues.

Constructivism also emphasizes the importance of cooperative work and of sharing ideas. If one person has a good idea then by sharing it with others all can gain and build new understanding. Therefore an important part of an inquiry-based activity is the communication of what was found. Students should be made to give talks, presentations, make posters etc.

This stage of the inquiry investigation gives the students the chance to justify the conclusions they have made. Students should be able to explain why they made their conclusions and why they believe they are correct. Students should be asked why they believe their results and conclusions are correct, what limitations there were to the experiment, and how it could be made better.

Poster making, giving talks, making models and objects

Giving a talk or making a poster is a good way to tell people what you are doing. It enables you to communicate your results and to get feedback. Because doing both these things takes a considerable amount of time and preparation, it forces you to think about what you have done and to make sure you understand fully what you have done means.

Ask students to design and make a poster, give a talk, draw a picture, or make an object or model. This is much more fun and creative, and more realistic than asking students to answer questions from a textbook or worksheet.

Discussion

Normally at a science conference when someone has just given a talk about an experiment they have done or something new they have found they end by asking the audience if they have any questions. This is the start of a small discussion in which the audience has the chance to probe the presenter about his experiment and his conclusions. Discussion is an important part of science that allows ideas to be spread, results to be challenged and opinions to be formed. Discussion allows communication between scientists and means new questions can be generated.

At the end of their work students should also have the chance to discuss what they found. You can initiate a small discussion with the class simply by asking questions to which students can reply, later students can take an active part in the discussion and raise questions of their own, either to other class members and other groups or to the teacher. When the students are forced to raise questions of their own they are forced to think about the work they or their colleagues did. Provide questions and ideas to keep the discussion going. A discussion gives the teacher the opportunity to judge what the students have learnt in the lesson and also allows the students to reinforce what they have just learnt.

<u>A flow chart of inquiry:</u>
You can ask students to create a flow chart showing the order in which they did things in the inquiry investigation. While making the flow chart the students learn to think about what they did and learn to evaluate the merits of what they did.

Adding relevance to the student's life

Can you remember some of the things that you found particularly difficult to remember at school? I always had problems learning the important parts of the periodic table and remembering the cycle of photosynthesis. It is difficult to remember things if they are abstract and seem to have no connection to you or your everyday life. It is much easier to remember things if you can somehow relate them to the objects and events you see around you everyday. Students will find it much easier to learn if they see the relevance of what they are being told. Provide examples of how the information developed in the lesson is used and seen in everyday life. If possible this should be done throughout the science lesson, but if this cannot be done then at the very least it should be mentioned at the end stage of the lesson.

For example if the students have been studying the water cycle they could look for various ways in which rainwater is collected and what happens to used water and where it goes. If you have been studying the physics of sound, then students should try to find out how a telephone works. If you have been studying electricity for homework students could list all the objects in there house that use electricity. Many students find science boring and irrelevant, to counter this it is important that students are made to see the real life effects of science around them.

Moving towards more open inquiry

In the first chapter of this book you may remember that different ways of classifying inquiry-based science were introduced. Lessons based on inquiry can occur at different levels of openness, depending on the extent to which the teachers or students are allowed to make decisions and control the learning in the classroom. You may remember that an inquiry matrix was given showing how inquiry was a continuum and that lessons became more open as the students were allowed to control each stage of the science lesson. Now you have seen what inquiry-based science lessons looks like and some of the ways in which a teacher can promote inquiry in the classroom you may be wondering how you could scaffold lessons and help students progress from low level forms of inquiry to more open and advanced of inquiry. How can you help students work independently?

One way to do this is to use a Science Inquiry Planning Framework (Fradd & Lee 1999, Fradd et al. 2001). This framework is meant to act as a scaffold, giving the students guidance, without actually telling them what to do. The Inquiry Framework makes the process of inquiry clear for students who have a poor background and understanding of science. While it provides a guide, it still allows openness. Ceuvas et al. (2005) found it provides a useful first step for teachers and students trying to learn and use the steps of the scientific process.

The Inquiry Framework

1. Questioning	State the problem

	• What do you want to find out? (written in the form of a question) **Make a hypothesis** • What do you think will happen?

2. Planning	**Make a plan by asking these questions** (think, talk, write)
	  α. What materials will I need?
	  β. What procedures or steps will I take to collect information?
	  χ. How will I observe and record results?

3. Implementing	**Gather the materials** • What materials do I need to implement my plan? **Follow the procedures** • What steps do I need to take to implement my plan? **Observe and record the results** • What happens after I implement my plan? • What do I observe? • How do I display my results? (using a graph, chart, table)
4. Concluding	**Draw a conclusion** • What did I find out? • Was my hypothesis supported by the evidence?
5. Reporting	**Share my results (informal)** • What do I want to tell others about the activity? **Produce a report (formal)** • Record what I did so others can learn • Consider different ways to express my information

A 10-point inquiry checklist: Is my lesson inquiry-based?

The following is a short checklist of questions that is designed to act as a guide to help you decide if your lesson really is inquiry-based or not. The ideal inquiry-based lesson where you could answer 'yes' to all these questions probably does not exist. It is impossible to incorporate everything into a lesson due to time constraints, the nature of the topic being studied, or the experiment being used. Some experiments are suitable for some aspects of inquiry and not for others. However, this checklist is meant to act as a rough guide to show if you are heading in the right direction.

Some points are more important in deciding whether the lesson is inquiry-based than others. For example the third and fifth questions should really be answered in the affirmative in any lesson that is hoping to be inquiry-based. On the other hand the points raised in the last few questions could be omitted and the lesson could still be inquiry rich. How many can you answer with a 'yes'?

- Do students work to try to find the answer to a scientific question or problem?
- Is a testable hypothesis or prediction made at the planning stage of the lesson?
- Do students design a 'method' and decide how to set the experiment up?
- Do students collect their own data, results or other information?
- Are students asked to make a conclusion from the information they have collected?
- Do students check whether the initial hypothesis or prediction was correct?
- Do students have to explain limitations and problems with the experiment that might affect the results they collected?
- Are students asked whether they might have made another conclusion if they had used a different method, had different data, or had different equipment?
- Are students asked to communicate their results to others, through writing, speech, or drawing?
- Are students asked to give the reasons and justify why they believe the conclusion they have made is correct?

GOOD TEACHER QUESTIONING

The whole of science is nothing more than a refinement of everyday thinking.

Albert Einstein

Good questioning by the teacher is the backbone of a good inquiry-based science lesson. Questions are the dynamo that propels an inquiry-based lesson forwards. As will have become apparent from reading the previous chapters many of the stages of inquiry require you to prompt students to find questions, develop ideas and think about what they are doing. Much of this prompting is done through questioning. Instead of telling the students what to do directly with specific instructions, you have to be able to give indirect guidance through the questions that you ask.

In this chapter questioning as a skill will be looked at. Ways in which you can improve your skill at asking questions, and how you can learn to ask the right types of question to promote inquiry will be covered. Later ways in which you can get students to ask questions will also be considered.

When should you be asking questions in the inquiry classroom?

This is an easy question to answer. You should be asking questions all of the time! However, the type of questions you ask should vary depending on which stage of the inquiry process the students are at. It is difficult to tell you exactly which questions you should be using; each lesson and experiment is different and lends it self to different questions. However, generally speaking the questions you ask should be prompting students to use certain skills at certain times of the lesson. Below is a rough guide of the type of questions you should be asking and when, which you can be use as a general guide. Choose which questions you ask to suit what you are trying to get students to do.

Questions to ask in the introduction phase

At the beginning of the inquiry lesson you should be asking questions which force students to look more carefully at what you give them to examine and which make them think about what they see happening. You should not be asking questions that test students' knowledge. Good questions to ask at this stage include:

- Have you seen?
- Did you notice?
- What did you see?
- What happened?

Resist the temptation to tell students what is happening or to give them 'the right answer.' Students may at this stage provide wrong answers or have false ideas. Wrong answers should not be corrected. These misconceptions should hopefully be ironed out during the course of the inquiry investigation. Remember this stage is simply about getting the students interested in the topic being taught and in finding out what ideas they have.

Questions to ask in the question and hypothesis generation phase

In this stage of the inquiry-based lesson you are trying to get students to produce their own questions that can then be used to form the basis of an investigation. This is a difficult task for which a standard list of suitable questions cannot be given. Teachers have to feel what is the right question to ask. A good first step is to try to narrow the topic being talked about down and to concentrate on one specific aspect. Good questions to ask at this stage include:

- What could you do to find out?
- What questions do you have?
- What happened when?

Questions to ask of students in the planning stage

The following questions are suitable to ask in the planning stage of an inquiry-based lesson:

- What could we do to find out?
- What do you think will happen if we change?
- What do you predict?
- What things could change in the experiment?
- What should we keep the same? What should we change? What will we record?
- What effect will this have?

In the planning stage you want students to think ahead and work out how they can do an experiment. You also want them to be making predictions and guesses about what might happen.

Questions the teacher should be asking during experimentation:
During experimentation ask questions like:

- What happens when you?
- Can you think of any other way of?
- What else could cause that?
- How is this the same/different from?

These questions force students to think about what they are doing and look at different possibilities open to them while they are experimenting.

Questions the teacher should ask in the interpretation stage
At this stage of inquiry ask the "why" and "how" questions, which should have been avoided in earlier sections of the lesson. Questions beginning with "why" and "how" are known as 'reasoning' questions (Elstgeest, 1985) and they prompt students to communicate their ideas and the reasons they have for these ideas. These questions are more suitable for use in this section of the lesson because the student should by now have some way of answering them; they have gained experience of the topic they are being asked about in the experimentation phase. The fact that students have some evidence to back up their answers should give them more confidence at answering these types of questions. Go on to ask other questions that prompt students to look at the data they have. Is there a pattern in the data? What does this table/graph/diagram show? What problems did they have?

Questions which you could ask at this stage of inquiry include:
- Can you explain why?
- Why do you think?
- How do you think it works?
- Why does this happen?

An example of good teacher questioning

Christian, a teacher at a German middle school, was teaching the physics of free falling bodies during one science lesson. Although this lesson was not pure inquiry, it was heading in that direction, and is a good example of how a good teacher uses questioning to help students think of ideas themselves.

The lesson began with Christian simply throwing a tennis ball back and forth between his students. This got his students attention. However, he did not do this in silence, he continually asked questions to get his students to try to describe how the tennis balls 'flew' and fell. 'What happens to the tennis ball when I throw it?' 'In what way does it move through the air?' 'What happens to the ball once it leaves my hand?' One female student tried to answer. 'The ball flies in a kind of arc after leaving your hand until it hits the ground.'

'What if I throw the ball really hard so that it flies horizontally?' asked Christian 'Will it carry on flying like this forever?' 'Why not?' Christian was probing his students to find out what they already knew about how things fell. He was making them think about something they normally took for granted and did not think about. He was not testing them, he wanted them to describe what they saw as he threw the balls.

The question the students were going to work with was written on the board. How do things fall? It would have been relatively easy for Christian to get students to come up with this question if he had prompted them. Christian wanted his class to conduct an experiment where they would measure how water falls in an arc from a hose. Galileo discovered the law of falling bodies using the same technique. However, how could Christian direct his students to think of this? With questioning of course! 'We want to measure and record how something falls. However, how can we do this? The tennis balls move too quickly to study properly. How can we make falling visible?'

The students had lots of good ideas. They suggested using slow motion photographs, or video cameras with slow motion functions. Christian listened to these ideas, and then turned a tap on in the room. 'Of course', said one female student, 'we can use water!' The students with Christians help soon constructed a suitable experimental set up. A hose was placed on a stand, so that a jet of water would fall out in a wide arc when the tap was turned on. A bucket was used to try to catch the water. The water was turned on and a falling arc of water was produced. Again Christian was directing the lesson with questioning. 'What happens when you turn the tap on more? Why? How does the water fall? Is this what you expected?'

Next Christian prompted the students to take some results. 'How can we measure how the water falls?' he asked. A pair of students tried directly measuring the stream of water and got wet. Christian again prompted the students; he turned on the overhead projector so a shadow was cast on the board of the water stream. The students now realized they could simply trace the arc of water as it fell onto the board. This the students now did.

Christian drew an axis around the arc drawn on the board and added numbers to it to make it into a graph showing the distance fallen against the distance traveled horizontally. Below the arc he drew a table showing the distance fallen against distance traveled. Christian explained that the amount of distance traveled horizontally actually corresponded to the time the water spent falling. The water traveled at a constant speed as it left the hose.

The graph and tables showed that in the first unit of time the water fell one unit of distance, in the second unit of time it had fallen 4 units of distance, and in the third second it had fallen 9 units of distance. Now Christian could use questioning to prompt the students to think about these numbers and what they meant. Could the students see a pattern? Could any student describe the relationships between the distance fallen and the time? How far did the students think the water would fall after 5 seconds? The students answered that the distance fallen increases as the square of the time. After 5 seconds the water would have fallen 25 units of distance. The students had discovered the basic principle behind the formula for falling bodies; namely $S = \frac{1}{2} g t^2$, without Christian telling them but simply by asking them questions.

Questioning tips:

<u>Ask higher level questions</u>

The type of question that is asked is very important. Benjamin Bloom (1956) created a classification scheme for questions, which depended on the thought abilities that different questions promoted. This scheme is shown in the table below. There is an increase in the complexity and thought needed in the questions as you move down the table. Those questions that require little thought or understanding are known as low level questions, while those that do are known as higher level questions.

Most questions asked by teachers and in school books tend to be knowledge or comprehension based. These questions test the student's ability to recall information, or ask the student to retell something in their own words. Knowledge and comprehension questions are considered to be low level in that students have to do little analysis or thought to answer them. More high-level questions include application, analysis and synthesis questions. These ask students to actually work something out, spot the relationships between things or create new ideas. These questions promote higher thinking. In an inquiry lesson the teacher should aim to use more high-level questions. Although knowledge and comprehension questions are not necessarily bad, there should be a good mix of all types of questions to promote different levels of thought in the students.

<u>Ask more open-ended questions</u>

Related to the last point is the use of closed and open-ended questions by the teacher. Most of the questions teachers ask tend to be closed. There is only one single correct answer. Open-ended questions to which there is no single correct answer are good for promoting higher thought skills in students, to initiate discussion, and to increase student participation.

A Representation of Blooms' Taxonomy:

Type of question	Skills used by Students	Examples
Knowledge	• Knowledge of facts and information. • Identifying. • Remembering and recalling information. • Recognizing.	Who? What? When? Where? How? List. Define. Tell. Describe. Identify. Collect.
Comprehension	• Understanding Information. • Translating knowledge into a new context/ from one medium to another. • Selecting facts. • Predict consequences infer causes.	Retell. Describe. Summarize. Predict. Distinguish. Interpret. Discuss, in your own words.
Application	• Use of information. • Problem solving. • Applying information.	Apply. Calculate. Illustrate. Show. Experiment. Discover. Classify. Why is…significant? How is…related to…?
Analysis	• Seeing patterns. • Subdividing to see parts. • Identifying components. • Recognition of hidden meaning.	Classify. Arrange. Connect. Explain. Divide. What are the parts of…? How does…contrast with…? What evidence can you find for…?
Synthesis	• Making new ideas from old ones. • Combining ideas.	How would you design? What ideas can you add? What solutions can you find? Rearrange. Modify. Substitute. Create. Formulate…?
Evaluation	Making values decisions about arguments and issues. Making choices based on arguments. Development of opinions, judgments etc.	Do you agree? What do you think about? Which do you think is most important? Assess, Decide, Rank, Discriminate, Judge, Support…?

Methods to increase the effectiveness of teacher questioning:

Increasing 'Wait Time'

Wait times are the short pauses that occur when a question is asked and an answer is given. There are two types of wait time. The first is the time gap between you asking a question and then asking someone to answer it. The second is the time gap after someone has answered your question and your response to the answer. Research has shown that increasing wait time is extremely beneficial (Rowe 1987). Most teachers have a wait time of only a second or so. Increasing this to around 3 seconds has some dramatic changes. More students will be willing to solicit an answer, student answers are typically longer, the quality of answers increases and confidence increases.

- Respond correctly to students answers

When a student responds to a question you pose make sure you listen to what the student has to say. Do not interrupt the student or cut them off as they are answering. Make sure you acknowledge the contribution the student has made. There are a number of ways of doing this. You can simply thank or praise the student, you can ask the student to elaborate on their answer, or you can repeat or rephrase what the student has said. If a student answers a question incorrectly, respond by correcting the student's ideas, or by elaborating on a correct part of what a student said. Try not to make students worried about answering questions incorrectly.

- Careful directing of questions/ the choice of a student to respond

Think carefully before you ask a question of who you want to answer it. You will probably find that if you ask questions to the whole class the same few students will raise their hand and want to respond. Try to increase participation by directing questions to students who would be less inclined to suggest an answer. Try to keep the class 'on its toes', ask a question before choosing the student you wish to respond so that everyone listens. Be careful you are not being biased in how you choose students to answer questions. It has been shown that teachers tend to prefer to ask male students to respond to questions in the science classroom. Try to counter this by directing a significant proportion of questions to female students.

Ways to get students to ask questions in the inquiry-based lesson

Self-questioning is an important skill necessary for students to problem-solve, in the building of knowledge, and in changing conceptions (Chin 2001). The questions which students ask can tell teachers much about student's level of thinking and understanding. One study found that reading comprehension increased in students taught to ask questions about the text they were reading (Koch & Eckstein 1991).

However, students ask relatively few questions, and the questions they do ask tend to be low-level questions that do not help develop understanding (Dillon 1988). Unfortunately students are usually conditioned by the school system not to ask questions, but rather to simply answer them

(Koch 2000). While reading this book you have probably noticed that getting students to produce questions is an important part of an inquiry-based science lesson. But how can you do this?

Methods to get students to ask questions;

- Make the asking or production of questions by the students a specific task during the introduction stage of inquiry. When introducing a topic, stop and ask students to write down 3 questions they have, and then choose some students to read out their questions to the class. Or if you show the students a phenomenon, afterwards ask students to pose questions about the demonstration to you. Write these questions on the board. Questions generated in these ways can be used as starting points for inquiry.

- Introduce question breaks into the inquiry lesson. Stop the lesson at unexpected times and ask students to write down three questions they have about the work they are doing. These questions can be about a problem they have with the experiment or topic. They give you the chance to see what students understand if they are having problems at that stage of inquiry and it helps them understand better what they are doing.

- Use question brainstorming, this is like normal brainstorming but questions are generated and not ideas.

- As part of homework ask students to produce questions about a specific topic. Give students newspapers or science magazine articles to read and then make questions. These questions can be used in the next lesson.

- At the end of an inquiry investigation ask the students as a matter of course what other things they would like to know in order to improve their experiments. 'What questions would you like answered which would help you improve your experiment?'

- Get students to write a 'science journal', as part of which they should fill in 'I wonder….' statements when they come across something which interests them.

- Encourage peer questioning: Before class discussions at the end of lessons ask students to think of questions that they could ask their colleagues about the work they have done. The discussion can then be kept going, by you the teacher asking students what question a student has and who they would like to pose it to.

MANAGING THE INQUIRY CLASSROOM

The man of science has learned to believe in justification, not by faith, but by verification.

Thomas H. Huxley

You need to be able to effectively manage the students in your classroom whatever method of teaching you use. You need to be in control of the class and must be able to create an atmosphere where study is possible and discipline maintained. A teacher who does not have adequate control over the class will not have much success teaching them, whatever method of teaching they use.

In more lecture style lessons it is relatively easy for teachers to keep the students in order. The students typically sit in rows facing the teacher. You are able to observe each and every student for most of the time. You are the one who does most of the speaking; when students do talk it is mainly to reply to you and not to talk with each other. In this way socializing between students is minimized during class time.

However, an inquiry-based lesson provides a much greater challenge for the teacher in terms of class management. In an inquiry-based lesson your students are given a certain amount of freedom and time to decide what they wish to do. Inquiry-based teaching emphasizes cooperative learning where students can spread ideas through group work and discussion with other class members. In an inquiry-based lesson you do not stand at the front of the class and observe everyone at once, but rather you have to move around the class offering support, as it is needed. These conditions mean students have a much greater opportunity to socialize in class, to do other things other than the work they are supposed to be doing, and to escape the notice of the teacher and 'lark around'.

Problems teachers face in managing inquiry-based classrooms

Lawson (2000) studied the problems newly trained teachers had in managing an inquiry classroom. Below are the most important problems that he found teachers having:

- There is a lack of student participation in inquiry activities.
- Students do not know how to do the inquiry work, they are unsure how to get started, lack sufficient background knowledge or do not want to have to think for themselves.
- The students have no interest in doing the inquiry-based project.
- Students talk at inappropriate times and fail to listen.
- Students are disruptive, bored or inattentive.
- Students socialize during the lesson.

Some of the lesser problems Lawson found included that some students want to participate too much, some students do not clean up after the lesson and leave early, and some students cheat and plagiarize other students work. To a certain extent some of these problems are present whatever the method of teaching is used. However, if you are to teach using inquiry successfully it is important that you have a good idea of how to combat these problems.

Lack of student participation
We all know that group work offers the perfect opportunity for the confident leader type students to take control of the group and to make the decisions and do most of the work, while the shyer less dominant individuals seem happy to take a back seat and contribute nothing. In class discussion it is easy for a student who does not wish to take part not to. You need to work hard to ensure everyone is included:

- Make sure groups have no more than 2 or 3 students, any larger and it offers the chance for some students to become passive group members.
- Direct questions carefully during class discussion to ensure that all students have the chance to participate.
- Assign each group member a specific task. If everyone in the group has been given a specific task then it stops one individual becoming dominant and means no one gets left out. Consider using job titles, for example 'Data recorder', or 'Group presenter,' and ask groups to choose who will be what.

Students do not know how to 'do' inquiry
Students who have not used inquiry much before may have problems working with it. In this case you must ensure you provide a clear and definite structure for the investigation and do not just leave students to flounder. It could be that you are expecting too much from the students and that the inquiry activity is too difficult. If this is the case provide more assistance to the students to make the task easier. Providing students with something like the inquiry framework can help them to see the structure of the inquiry lesson and help students decide what they need to do next.

The area in which the students are most likely to have problems is at the beginning, when they have to find a problem, and then develop a question and hypothesis. If this is too difficult for the students provide the information the students need, or prompt them to find what they need so that they can continue with the investigation.

Students may lack the required background knowledge to conduct some inquiry investigations. Try to plan inquiry activities well so that students will not be given activities that are beyond them. As Colburn (2000) says, inquiry activities need to be 'just right', in terms of difficulty, too hard and students will not be able to complete them, too easy and students will not be challenged and will become bored.

Students may not want to have to think for themselves; you might hear comments like 'just give me the answer.' Inquiry is more challenging for students than other methods of teaching, and students should be made to continue with inquiry and not simply be told what to do. In the end the students will see the benefit of having to decide what to do themselves and will gain increasing independence. Although at the beginning inquiry may seem hard, with increasing practice the students will find it more interesting and fun than traditional activities.
Do not give in or give up!

The students see no relevance in doing the inquiry-based project
In previous chapters it has been emphasized how important it is to make science relevant to the lives of the students. Work hard at showing how a specific topic affects them. Sometimes this is difficult with more abstract projects, but normally the relevance of the experiment can be shown at the end of the investigation during the period of discussion. Try to link the work that you give students to do with their lives. This can be done for most projects studied through inquiry-based learning. For example an inquiry-based lesson about light bulb circuits explain that the same principles are used in lighting systems in their own homes. If you make the effort to make these connections your students will be more motivated and will learn better.

Students talk at inappropriate times and fail to listen
As you probably know, it can be difficult keeping control of the class when it is working in scattered groups around the classroom. When wanting to talk to the class try to be dominant and in control, try to get the attention of the class, and then wait until everyone has stopped talking before you begin to talk. Remember that students have only a short attention span, and therefore if you talk for any length of time you will start to lose their attention. Keep your points short and too the point and do not waffle.

Students are disruptive, bored or inattentive
As Lawson (2000) points out these problems are caused mainly when the tasks given to students are at an inappropriate level for them. Students will become bored and disruptive if the work they are doing is too difficult for them or too easy. This problem is made worse because often classes are made up of students of wide ability, and thus finding an activity suitable for them all can be difficult. The solution is to try to tailor tasks for students of different abilities. Students of high ability should be given more challenging titles and problems to investigate, and be given less

support by the teacher. Students of lesser ability should be given more help, and the inquiry-base activity should be simplified to allow them to work using it.

Students will become bored and disruptive if they have no set time frames in which to work. If students feel they 'have all lesson' they will be more likely to waste time and thus become bored and disruptive. Set time limits in which specific tasks have to be completed.

Students socializing during class

The more free time that your students have during lessons, the more time they will spend talking and socializing with each other instead of actually doing their work (Sampson 2004). There are a number of possible ways to combat this problem (Lawson 2000, Sampson 2004):

- Give students a specific time frame in which to complete their work. If you tell students they only have 5 minutes to plan their experiments before you begin questioning them, they will be more likely to actually begin work. If they believe they have unlimited time they will be more likely to socialize first.
- Circulate around the class observing and posing questions to the groups. Do not simply sit at your desk 'to do some marking.' If students see you retreat to your desk they will take this as a sign that they can do what they want.

Meeting Teachers Who Use Inquiry

Chad Williams teaches science to 6th through to 8th grade students at the Potomac Elementary School, Bonner, Montana. He has a keen interest in inquiry-based teaching.

"Inquiry means that the teacher places trust in the student to seek an answer themselves. The key to this is having a hook that gets the students interested. What I mean by this is that instead of thinking about what the teacher is going to do, the students must start with an end objective in mind. Then the students can build backwards with this goal as the conclusion. Inquiry is a way of teaching that presents the overlying objectives to the student in the form of a question. Then with some guiding questions I most often turn the lesson or project into an investigation. This is then guided with many questions as I circulate through the room as the student's investigate the problem placed before them.

At times I pull them all back together for some clarification while always encouraging them to think outside of the box. I have found that by using this method they many times go farther and deeper into a subject than I would have directed them. The real trick is keeping your excitement up so that it is contagious with the students. The other trick is to not show the teachers fright of letting go of some of the control in the classroom.

Inquiry can be hard at first but I have found it to be really rewarding for both the student and myself. My passion is science so I have been extremely motivated in implementing it into my sixth, seventh and eighth grade science classes. Getting inquiry right is a lot of trial and error. The key is to have an end goal in place and to instill trust in your students that they are capable of learning. Some lessons will go better than others but in order to grow failure has to be part of the mix.

Teachers need to find the balance of control between the teacher and the students for Inquiry to work. During inquiry the class is not without guidance, just that in inquiry some of the responsibility of seeking out the answers is placed in the hands of the student. I have found that the students involved in inquiry-based learning excel farther than those placed in a strict teacher controlled classroom setting.

I think one reason inquiry is not used more in classrooms is the discomfort to the teacher of giving up some of the classroom control. Also many teachers have come to the conclusion that when they are in their classroom with the door closed it is easier to do the same lesson in the same way they have done for the last 15 years. I think it is good to shake things up ever couple of years. Anther problem is with administrators who are unfamiliar with inquiry, and who often think that a quiet classroom with straight rows where the teacher dominates is fantastic. These administrators are missing the chance to bring creativity into their schools."

Meeting Teachers Who Use Inquiry

Bonnie Glasgold is an elementary and middle school science teacher from Brooklyn, New York. She has been teaching for 21 years. She employs a hands-on approach to the teaching of science. She has written numerous articles about classroom management.

Author: What does inquiry-based science mean to you?
BG: Inquiry based science means learning by asking questions.

Author: Name a topic you have taught using inquiry. What did the students do? What experiment did they conduct?

BG: An experiment I did recently was for children to find out about the volume of water. We wondered why the same amount of water looked like different amounts when placed in different size containers (tall, wide, long, etc). From this inquiry based experiment, the children were to measure the same amount of water (100ml) into each of the different shaped jars. They then measured the water line and marked it with masking tape or a marker. They were able to see that the shape of the container was the reason why the volume looked different. From this they concluded that water takes the shape of the container (a property of liquids). This was all based on inquiry.

Author: How would you suggest that other teachers start using inquiry? What is a good way to start?

BG: Teachers need to teach inquiry thinking. They need to teach the basics; like comparison, prediction, contrast, observation, and the tools scientists use to go with inquiry based thinking; pan balances, forceps, scales, spring scale, measuring tapes, rulers, hand lens, magnifiers, etc. This gives students a way to explore and find out things.

Author: Many teachers are scared of losing control in inquiry-based lessons and giving the students too much freedom. How do you keep in control?

BG: I find that control isn't a problem as long as you have established the rules and routines first. Children must know how to work in groups, how to get materials, how to talk (in low voices) and how to use all of the tools. These must be consistently reinforced by the teacher and modeled. The teacher should begin by modeling all that he/she wants from the students.

Author: How do you organise inquiry in your classroom? Do students work in groups? How do you structure the lessons?

BG: I try to have my students work in groups of four; that's not too big or too small. The groups are mixed abilities; and each child is encouraged to participate. I might assign roles; like reporter, recorder, materials, etc: or let them choose on their own. I usually model the experiment to some degree, enough so they know how to proceed, and them walk around and coach or facilitate as they are working, always asking questions about what they are doing and what they are observing.

Author: How do you stop students becoming bored, disruptive? How do you tailor lessons for students of different ability?

BG: Lessons are tailored for students of different ability by having them in heterogeneous groups, where they may play a role that they are suited for. For example, a student may not write or verbalize well, but can draw- they will be the group artist. I always help the slower learners by giving them more attention or helping them verbalize what they are thinking and then writing their verbal answers down. I find most children can think better than write! When the children lose interest, I simply stop the experiment: ask the problem, would they like to continue, what have we learned, are we finished? This usually gets them back on task.

EVALUATION AND ASSESSMENT

Research! A mere excuse for idleness; it has never achieved, and will never achieve any results of the slightest value.

Benjamin Jowett

One of the most important jobs you have to do while teaching your classes is to assess your students. You need to find out what students have learnt, how much progress they have made, and how hard they have worked. Assessment of students allows you to identify problems students may have and areas of general weakness. The assessment of students is especially important in the modern classroom, where often stringent targets are set by curricula and governing bodies which proscribe what should be learnt and when. Formal examination is now common at regular intervals throughout a child's education and good assessment is important in ensuring that students are well prepared for this.

Two different types of assessment:

Summative Assessment
As its name suggest summative assessment is assessment that takes place at the end of learning. In summative assessment the teacher makes judgments about what the student has learned while studying a topic. A typical form of summative assessment would be an 'end test' conducted at the end of a week learning a specific science topic.

Formative Assessment
Formative assessment on the other hand refers to the gathering and use of information about students' ongoing learning and is used to modify teaching and learning activities (Harlen 2003). Assessment can occur throughout the time of learning and is used to direct further teaching. When teachers discover where students are having problems, they can vary instructional techniques,   re-teach,   or   give   opportunities   for   further   practice.

95

A comprehensive study by Black and William (1998) found that formative assessment has a positive effect on student learning and increases student scoring on summative testing. The feedback which students get through formative assessment seems to help them identify their weak points and to strengthen them.

Evaluation in a non-inquiry classroom; Summative assessment testing for knowledge learnt

The aim of traditional non-inquiry lessons is to teach knowledge to students. The best way to assess whether students have learnt this knowledge is to use summative assessment once a topic has been taught. You are probably familiar with the main form of assessment used in non-inquiry lessons, that of simple testing. This is where students are given a short test to find out what knowledge they have gained about a topic or subject. These tests are often formal.

Another form of assessment that you probably did a lot of yourself at school is the answering of questions that are given in class or as homework. Questions are often obtained from school textbooks or worksheets. The students' ability is judged according to their ability at being able to answer these questions. This type of assessment is non-formal.

Another commonly used way of assessing students in a traditional science setting is the 'experimental write-up'. You must simply mark student's lab reports or experiments that they have done in class. This method of assessment is the closest to actually assessing student's science process skills. Lab reports are often written in the 'introduction, method, results, and conclusion' format, mirroring the way scientists write up their work in journals.

The danger with all these methods of assessment are that they do not necessarily assess the level of understanding a student has. The answers for a test can be memorized without any real comprehension as to there meaning on the part of the student. Experimental write-ups can follow exactly the instructions the student was given and the result the student was told to find, but do not mean the student understands why they did the procedure or what they discovered. With traditional methods of assessment the knowledge of the student is assessed and not necessarily their ability at using the science process skills.

Evaluation in the Inquiry Classroom; Formative Assessment testing for understanding

While in a non-inquiry classroom the main aim is to give the students knowledge, in the inquiry classroom there are mixed aims. A teacher in an inquiry classroom of course wants their students to gain knowledge of the topic they are studying, but of much more importance is the fact that students build understanding. The ability of students to use science process skills is also of much more importance than in traditional non-inquiry lessons.

Formative assessment is built into inquiry-based science. If you are teaching using the inquiry-based way, you are teaching in a constructionist way, and thus are finding out what your students know and are learning throughout the learning process. The first step for a teacher in an inquiry classroom is to find out what prior knowledge the students have, and then to adapt teaching to this knowledge; this is formative assessment. Formative assessment is being used throughout the inquiry lesson, either by the teacher or the student. Whenever you have a class discussion, ask students questions, prompt students to think about their experiments students are being assessed in a formative way.

Ways to improve assessment

In a companion paper to their study on formative assessment Black & Williams give suggestions on ways of improving formative assessment in the classroom (Black & Williams 1998). Some of their ideas are summarized below.

Remove Grading: Nothing is more depressing and dispiriting than always obtaining low marks or grades. Students lose self-esteem and begin to believe they cannot improve. Grading or ranking students sets up a competition between students, and some students will inevitably be the losers. Students begin to look for easy answers and avoid difficult questions. Remove the fear of failure from the classroom and remove grading.

Allow students to assess themselves: The best people to assess students are the students themselves. They know what they have learnt. Tell students what goals or targets they had and ask them if they have reached them.

Give feedback: Students simply given grades do not learn anything. Students should be given guidance as to how to improve, and students must have the chance to put these improvements into practice.

Use testing as opportunities for learning: If students do tests or answer questions as homework, use this as an opportunity to provide feedback. Go over the questions with students and start a class discussion asking students what answers they think are correct and why.

Use regular short testing: Do not have single 'big' tests at the end of semesters. Have lots of 'mini' tests throughout the year. Keep tests short and relevant to what students have just learnt. Try to test students shortly after they have learnt about something, say about a week afterwards.

Integrate assessment into the lesson: Choose assessment tasks that become part of the lesson and are not seen as a separate 'test.' Choose activities for assessment carefully. Take care to choose tasks that allow students to express their understanding.

Have the right attitude: If you believe that some of your students will never do very well and can't improve then why are you wasting your time doing assessment? Some students will always struggle, but if you believe you can make a difference to them and help them improve, even slightly, then your assessment will be more productive and useful. Develop the belief that your assessment helps students improve their work.

Grading students in inquiry-based science lessons

It is all well and good to know that you are using formative assessment while you are teaching inquiry-based science, but this will not necessarily please parents and school directors. They want to know how much the students have learnt! They want grades, notes and marks. They want to know if their little Johnny has an A or a C. In other words, although formative assessment is an integral part of inquiry teaching, you need to be able to use the work done in an inquiry setting to produce grades and final assessments. You need to salvage some kind of summative assessment from the inquiry lesson. Some suggested methods for doing this are provided below:

Assessment of knowledge

As well as using the traditional methods of assessing knowledge learnt already described above, you can also use one of the following more modern methods during inquiry-based lessons:

- Posters: if students have to make a poster as part of their inquiry activity this can be used to assess their level of knowledge about the subject being studied.

- Discussion: a student's level of understanding can be found during a discussion. However the problem with this method is that it is nearly always impossible to assess all the students.

- Planning sheets/other inquiry-based worksheets: as part of many inquiry-based lessons students are required to fill in planning sheets, design sheets, or conclusion sheets. These can be used as the basis for assessment in much the same way as traditional lab reports.

Brainstorming: Students brainstorming activities can be used to assess what they have learnt in a lesson. Ask students to make a brainstorming about a topic that has just been studied, and then judge what the student has learnt by what they have and have not included on the brainstorming. Maybe a better way of using brainstorming as an assessment technique is to ask students to conduct a brainstorming at the beginning of learning about a topic, and then again at the end, and then assess the difference between the two to see how the student has progressed.

Assessing science process skills

Finding out whether someone can do something is generally more difficult than trying to find out if someone knows something. Nearly everyone can tell you the steps needed in driving a car: 'place in first gear, give some gas, raise the clutch, release the handbrake.' But how do you assess whether someone is a good driver or not? Many people argue that a short driving test is no indication of driving ability. So how can you assess whether someone is good at using the science process skills and is a competent scientist?

The methods below are suggested ways that can be used to assess student's ability and rate of progress with the process skills of science. These methods are therefore especially useful for use in an inquiry-based classroom.

Marking rubrics: A marking rubric is a list of experimental abilities. For each ability there are a number of different levels. You need to decide at which level the student is at by observing their work throughout the inquiry session. For example one ability could be planning. You must decide whether the student is poor, satisfactory, or very good at this skill. At each level there are examples of what the student has to show in order to be classed at that level. To obtain a very good; the student might have to show that he can 'plan and design experiments correctly and be able to find variables.' A design for a rubric suitable that you could use in an inquiry-based lesson can be seen on the following pages.

Holistic rubrics: As its name would suggest in a holistic rubric all of the criteria are assessed together and not separately as in a normal rubric. Instead of each criterion receiving a score or level, you decide on an overall score or level for the student depending on their overall achievement. The use of a holistic rubric is quicker and simpler than using a normal rubric, but does not allow you to do an exact analysis of separate students abilities. Therefore the use of holistic rubrics should be used only for general assessment and not to provide detailed information about student learning.

Checklists: When making a checklist you need to formulate a list of behaviors or skills that you hope to see a student use in the classroom. Then you tick off these skills if and when you see them being used by your students. Each student should have his or her own checklist. You have to decide when and how to observe students. You also need to decide for how long to observe students and at which stages of the lesson or experiment. Checklists are easy to use and design and provide a good picture of the skills that a student is using. However, they are difficult to make comprehensive and often do not give you a complete picture of your students abilities.

Posters: Having students produce a poster to explain how and why they conducted an experiment the way they did is much better than simply asking them to do a lab write-up for homework. Poster making allows students to work in groups, which means they will discuss and justify their ideas with each other. Students will take more pride in a poster than a normal lab write-up because posters provide students with the opportunity to present their work to other students. Posters can be used to assess both students knowledge about a specific topic and their ability at using science process skills in completing an experiment. Assess posters with the use of a checklist or rubric.

Science portfolios: Another often cited idea for assessing students is to use science portfolios. Throughout the term or year you ask student to keep all the work they have done. At the end of the term or year they then have to put together a portfolio of their work. They have to decide which work to include and which work to discard. They have to justify their decisions and why they feel that some work is better than other. You can then assess the science portfolio and the student's justifications using a rubric.

Multiple choice and standard testing: Although these are traditional methods of assessing students and mostly test for the learning and memorization of science content knowledge, they can also be used to assess student's knowledge of the science process skills. Questions should be formulated especially to test student's knowledge of science as inquiry.

Example questions for multiple-choice tests assessing process skills

Imagine you want to conduct an experiment to find out how the weight of a pendulum affects its rate of swinging. What things would you keep the same in your experiment, and what things would you change?

A: CHANGE: Length of string used. KEEP SAME: Weight of pendulum, angle at which pendulum starts.

B: CHANGE: Angle at which pendulum starts. KEEP SAME: Weight of pendulum, length of string used.

C: CHANGE: Weight of pendulum. KEEP SAME: length of string used for pendulum, angle at which pendulum starts.

You want to conduct an experiment to find out how different types of music affect plant growth. Which of the following would you do?

A: Collect together sunflower plants of the same age. Measure the size of the sunflowers before the experiment starts and label each plant. For the first week the plants will hear heavy metal music for one hour per day. The growth after one week will be recorded. In the second week the sunflowers will hear classical music for one hour per day, and after a week the growth will be recorded. In the third week the plants will hear no music and the growth will be measured after one week.

B: Collect together sunflower plants of the same age, label each plant, measure their size, and divide into 3 groups; A, B, C. Group A will have no music played to them. Group B will hear classical music. Group C will hear heavy metal. Each day each group will be taken to a separate room and have their music played at them for one hour. The growth of the plants will be measured every week.

C: Collect together sunflower plants and divide into 3 groups; A, B, C. Group A will have no music played to them. Group B will hear classical music. Group C will hear heavy metal. Each day each group will be taken to a separate room and have their music played at them for one hour. The height of the plants will be measured every week

Example test questions assessing students skills at the process skills

1. Design and plan an experiment to find out if objects of different weights and sizes fall to the ground at different speeds. Write down how you would do the experiment. What would you measure? What variables would you change and which would you keep the same?

2. A fellow scientist conducted an experiment to see how good different brands of thermos flask were at retaining heat. He has gone on holiday and left you to finish his report. His results are below. Decide on a suitable way to present these results. How can you make the results easy to interpret? Which flask do you think is best? Why?

Time after boiling water added	Temperature of liquid in flasks °C		
	Flask 1	Flask 2	Flask 3
15 minutes	88	79	67
30 minutes	80	74	54
45 minutes	74	71	46
60 minutes	68	65	41
75 minutes	57	63	35

An example of a holistic rubric

Grade 1:

The student is able to successfully develop a hypothesis and then plan an investigation that gives a priority to evidence without support from the teacher.

The student is able to record data accurately.

The student is able to formulate conclusions based on the evidence collected, and then justify these conclusions independently.

The student is able to work cooperatively with other class members successfully.

The student is able to present their work and justify their conclusions articulately.

Grade 2:

The student requires some prompting in order to develop a hypothesis and plan an investigation.

The student is able to record data accurately with some prompting.

The student is able to formulate conclusions based on the evidence and then justify these conclusions, but requires some prompting.

The student is able to work cooperatively.

The student is able to present their work and justify the conclusions made in a competent manner.

Grade 3:

The student needs substantial help in order to find a hypothesis and develop an investigation.

The student needs substantial support in order to record data.

The student has problems formulating conclusions and justifying them using the evidence. A large amount of help is needed.

The student is only able to work with others for short periods of time.

The student attempts to present their work, but does not justify their conclusions.

Grade 4:

The student was unable to find a hypothesis and develop an investigation, even with substantial support.

The student is unable to record data.

The student is unable to formulate conclusions on their own.

The student is unable to work with others.

The student has problems to present work.

10

WHY IS INQUIRY NOT USED MORE?

Men are born ignorant, not stupid. They are made stupid by education.

Bertrand Russell

Although inquiry-based science has been widely accepted as being a good method of teaching by science teacher educators for a number of years, the technique remains relatively little used in schools. There are a number of reasons why this might be so. Maybe one of the main hindrances to inquiry-based science are the curricula many school boards and teaching authority base their science education programs on. These are often content-orientated rather than process-orientated, encouraging the teaching of large amounts of factual knowledge instead of the teaching of science process skills and a basic understanding of science.

However, maybe the main reason why inquiry fails to be implemented in schools is because of the views and problems experienced by teachers using inquiry. Teachers see a number of problems with the use of inquiry-based science and these hinder its implementation (Deters 2005, Keys and Bryan 2001, Eick and Reed 2002). Some of these problems may be real, but others may only be perceived, or be used as an excuse for not implementing inquiry by teachers unwilling or worried about using the technique. In either case it is important that these problems are tackled and dealt with. The following problems with inquiry-based science were proposed by Deters (2005), Welch et al. (1981) and Eltinge and Roberts (1993).

Why teachers may be reluctant to use inquiry-based science:

Inquiry-based science takes more time
Teaching using traditional techniques can be quick. Because the lesson is teacher centered and the teacher is in control, the teacher has the opportunity to set the pace of the lesson. Simply lecturing students about what they need to know can cover a lot of material quickly. Providing

students with detailed methods sheets to use while experimenting and telling them what they should be looking for means experiments can be done in double quick time.

Unfortunately inquiry-based science can take much longer. As the students are in control they can set the pace of the lesson; a worrying thought for a teacher having curriculum targets to meet. Because the students are not told 'what to do,' but decide themselves, experimenting takes a much longer time. Planning for an inquiry-based lesson can also take longer than simply looking in the teaching manual accompanying a school textbook.

It is unfortunately difficult to solve this problem. Good time management can help. It is not necessarily to make every practical lesson inquiry-based, it has been shown that just doing several inquiry-based lessons over a year can have a significant effect on students. Time should be made for this.

The teacher loses control

A key feature of inquiry-based science is that students take control of the lesson; they decide what to do and how to do it. Many teachers are wary of losing control and would rather know exactly what is happening all the time in their lessons. There is a perception that when teachers do not 'lead' the students and students are allowed to decide for themselves the teacher is somehow not doing their job or is not very good.

Teachers need to realize that it there is nothing wrong with letting students work independently and that they are not being bad teachers by doing this. When students leave school they will have problems to solve on their own without anyone to help them, and it is best if they can practice these skills while still in school.

Problems with safety

Letting students conduct their own experiments? Surely a recipe for disaster! Visions of burnt down labs; electrocutions or explosions caused by mixing unsuitable chemicals together may come to mind. However such perceptions are generally unfounded. Inquiry-based science experiments are not generally any more dangerous than conventional ones. If students have to get their plans or ideas checked by the teacher before conducting them then any possible dangers can be avoided or minimized. A well prepared teacher should have a good idea of what might 'crop up' in any particular lesson and should be able to anticipate any safety problems and head them off easily.

Inquiry-based sessions might not 'work'

There is a danger in inquiry-based experiments that the experiments may fail, or that false or erroneous results may be collected and that students may 'get the wrong idea.' Teachers want experiments that are sure to succeed and that lead to students making a particular conclusion. Unfortunately real life science does not work like this and if students are to learn how science really works they have to experience what it is like to have an experiment fail, to collect false results, or to be misled. These negative aspects should not be seen as a disadvantage but as an important part of learning to become a scientist. If false ideas are formed teachers just have to work harder to correct them.

Lack of resources

Some teachers say they cannot conduct inquiry because they do not have sufficient resources. Inquiry-based work involves the use of much more equipment and in some schools there are simply not the resources available for this.

Many inquiry activities do not require expensive equipment and can be done quite simply. Students might like to have the resources available to build their own jet rocket for their inquiry project about flight, but like in the real world nobody has enough money for everything they want. Every scientist would like their own electron microscope, but this is not possible, and doesn't mean they can't do any research any more!

Some teachers comment that there are not enough examples of inquiry-based projects available for them to use. Ideas for inquiry experiments can be found in a variety of sources. The Internet contains a large number of ideas. There are a number of books containing ideas. Many teaching journals provide ideas for inquiry lessons. Traditional experiments can be adapted for inquiry using the ideas in this book.

Inquiry is only of value to high ability students

There is a perception amongst many teachers that inquiry-based science is only an effective technique for students of high academic ability. Many teachers consider that inquiry is not suitable for students of average or below average ability, and that if confronted with inquiry these students would be unable to work in this way.

It is easy to imagine how this idea originated. A teacher giving a fully open inquiry-based project to a class of students who had never seen it before would probably see that most of the students would have no idea how to work using inquiry. Only the very clever might be able to make a start, the rest would struggle. Such a teacher might then conclude that inquiry is only suitable for the brightest. This would be a mistake.

As mentioned time and time again in this book, inquiry needs to be introduced gradually to students. Teachers need to slowly help students use inquiry. Different aspects of inquiry need to be introduced when the students are ready. Although in inquiry-based science the student has to make more of the decisions, this does not mean the teacher has nothing to do. The teacher has to guide and help student reach independence. All students can work using inquiry-based science they just need proper support.

Student resistance to inquiry

When first introduced to inquiry-based science students might not think very much of it. It is easy to see why. Firstly they have to do more. They have to think. Students cannot simply sit in class and listen, they have to engage their minds and then do something. This takes effort. We are all a little bit lazy and we all complain if we have to work a little harder. Students are no exception. The 'just tell me the answer' phenomenon, where students simply want to be told what they need to know and not work it out for themselves is well known of in the inquiry setting. The answer is perseverance. Studies have shown that students who do use this technique find it ultimately more rewarding and more enjoyable than traditional techniques. Students develop feelings of self-confidence and self-satisfaction after being able to work independently. They just need forcing over that first difficult first hurdle.

Another student related problem is that of students not knowing how to do inquiry. At first students may be perplexed and not understand what they need to do, or how to do it. Students are scared of working alone. Once again introducing students to inquiry gradually helps minimize this problem. Teachers should first use lower level forms of inquiry, before getting students to use more open forms of inquiry. It is not fair to simply expect students to be able to complete a full open inquiry experiment when it is the very first time they have come across one. Teachers need to provide scaffolding to gradually help students get to open inquiry.

Lack of training and support

It is often the case that teachers feel they do not have sufficient training to conduct inquiry-based science themselves. Teachers may feel they do not understand inquiry-based science well enough to teach using it. Teachers wishing to use inquiry-based science may not receive the support required from colleagues or teaching assistants, who do not believe in the value of inquiry-based methods. The responsibility for this relies to a large extent on education researchers who have conflicting views of what inquiry is and what it should contain and who have failed to convince many teachers of the benefit of inquiry. Much of the research conducted into inquiry is purely theoretical and does not address the real concerns which teachers in the classroom have. This barrier can only be overcome with increasing awareness about inquiry and better teacher training schemes.

Difficulty of assessment

Most methods of assessing science ability and the effectiveness of science learning are based on the amount of scientific factual knowledge the student has gained, rather than assessing the students understanding and ability at using science process and inquiry skills. This is because it is much easier to assess students' knowledge of science, rather than test their ability and understanding of science. In an inquiry-based classroom students learn less factual knowledge, but are better able to use science process skills. Teachers who believe that students taught with inquiry-based science will do worse at factual assessment may be discouraged at using it. Methods of assessment promoting increased understanding of science should be encouraged in favor of factual based assessment methods.

Teachers views and attitudes as barriers to the use of inquiry-based science

Maybe the greatest barriers to the implementation of inquiry-based science are the teachers themselves. All teachers possess beliefs, ideas, and attitudes that affect how they teach (Eick and Reed, 2002, Keys and Bryan, 2001). Teachers with beliefs and attitudes which are at odds with those of inquiry-based science will have significant problems teaching using inquiry. They will not see the value of inquiry-based science and may not believe that it is an effective teaching method. Teachers who see inquiry as ineffective or not being worthwhile will probably quote some of the disadvantages of using inquiry mentioned above for not teaching with this method.

Inquiry-based science is based on the constructivist theory of learning. For teachers to appreciate the value of inquiry-based science they first need to understand how constructivism views the learner. Teachers possessing old fashioned or false views of how children learn will have problems teaching in an inquiry-based way (Tobin and McRobbie 1996). The first step is persuading teachers that inquiry-based science is useful is to help them to understand constructivism. Inquiry-based science is also based on the modern way of doing science. Teachers with old fashioned or outdated views of how science is conducted will have problems teaching using inquiry (Brickhouse 1990, Gallagher 1991). There is a wide range of teaching literature available that explains constructivism very well, and this could be used to help teachers develop more modern views of teaching.

Maybe the best way to change teachers' views is to get them to experience inquiry for themselves. A person's experience of using inquiry affects greatly how they view it (Windschtl 2003, Eick and Reed 2002). Student teachers given the opportunity to learn using inquiry-based science for the first time become exited and enthusiastic about the technique (Windschtl 2003, Marlow et al. 2003). They begin to view science differently and start to plan how they can use the technique themselves in their own classrooms when they begin to teach. Teachers with views and beliefs at odds with those of inquiry should be encouraged to take part in an inquiry-based science project themselves, by doing so they will understand how inquiry works and how powerful it can be.

Meeting the Science Teacher Educators

Barbara Crawford is an Associate Professor of Science Education at Cornell University, Ithaca. She researches ways to support prospective and practicing teachers in developing their knowledge and beliefs about scientific inquiry. She has written a number of papers examining teachers' views of inquiry, including 'Embracing the Essence of Inquiry: New Roles for Science Teachers' (2000) and 'Is it realistic to expect a preservice teacher to create an inquiry-based classroom?' (1999).

Author: How would you describe inquiry-based science? What is inquiry?

BC: First, inquiry is a natural way that we seek understanding about the world we live in. Second, I would describe inquiry-based science teaching as an instructional approach that engages students in investigating for themselves real-world problems in science. This approach involves designing a classroom environment that allows students time to ask and answer real-world science questions, in collecting and analyzing data, in developing possible solutions, building models, and discussing their ideas with other students in the classroom.

Author: What are the main advantages of inquiry-based science? What is it good at doing which traditional methods of teaching are not?

BC: Inquiry-based science teaching allows time and opportunity for students to learn important science concepts in-depth: not just memorizing facts, but also in developing their own understandings. Traditional science teaching (lecture, drill and practice, rote memorization) can be useful for learning skills and certain facts; but this type of learning environment does not support deep conceptual understanding and is not motivating to students.

Author: What role should inquiry-based science play in the classroom?

BC: Although this is not the only approach to teaching, I believe that inquiry-based science teaching should play a very big role. My agenda is to change the way science is taught in most science classrooms, to be more inquiry-based and student centered.

Author: How should teachers learn to teach inquiry-based science?

BC: I do not know the answer to this question. However, from my research in classrooms, teachers' sets of beliefs about science and learning play an important part in how teachers develop and carry out science instruction. It is important for a teacher to have had some experience in research, but this is not enough. A teacher needs to understand a bit about the philosophy, history, and sociology of science, and have seen models of this kind of teaching.

Author: What do you believe to be the greatest reason why teachers don't use inquiry in their classrooms?

BC: From my research, teachers need to hold beliefs about learning and about science that fit with this kind of teaching.

Author: What can teachers do when they want to become more inquiry orientated? How can they learn to become inquiry teachers?

BC: Teachers need to have some experience in research, they need to see some examples in classrooms of this kind of teaching, and they need to have the desire to teach in this way. Teachers themselves are the key to change.

Author: Many reasons are given for why teachers don't use inquiry. For example, a lack of time or resources, a need to cover the curriculum, lack of colleague support, and worries about losing control. Do you believe these are real problems that teachers need to overcome, or do you believe many teachers use them as excuses because they lack understanding or personal experience of inquiry?

BC: I do not blame teachers. Some of these are real problems. We now know that this kind of teaching is very challenging. It is not easy. Most importantly, teachers may not have had opportunity to learn science in inquiry-based ways-they themselves had not had the experiences as learners to understand how scientists learn about the world. Teachers can join other teachers and professionals and form learning communities, and work in a group to address these issues.

Meeting the Science Teacher Educators

Brenda Capobianco is an assistant professor of science education at Purdue University, West Lafayette. Her research interests include engaging teachers in action research and studying how teachers affect women's participation in science, technology, and engineering. She is a member of the editorial board for the Journal of Science Teacher Education.

Author: What does inquiry-based science mean to you?

BC: Inquiry has been a broadly defined construct in science education. It has been associated with a wide range of intellectual activities, including hypothesis testing, practical problem-solving, modeling, and engaging Socratic dialogue to name just a few examples. Our program entitled "Building Excellence in Science Teaching through Inquiry" (BESTI) is a teacher professional development program that refers to inquiry in which questions about the natural world are posed, hypotheses are generated, investigations are designed, and data are collected and analyzed in order to resolve the question.

 Author: What do teachers and students do in an inquiry-based lesson?

BC: The role of the science teacher in a science inquiry-based lesson is that of a facilitator. The science teacher is asking productive questions, encouraging students to ask testable questions, and facilitating their learning through inquiry.

Author: Why is it better than traditional methods?

BC: Inquiry is not necessarily "better than traditional methods". It is an approach that is effective at encouraging students to explore natural phenomena through authentic investigations and to develop conceptual understanding of science through structured, guided, or independent explorations.

Author: Many teachers are worried about using inquiry thinking they might lose control if students are allowed to make decisions in the classroom. Is this a true problem?

BC: This question is centered on the concern for how much structure and/or freedom teachers should provide in inquiry-oriented science. The type and amount of structure can vary depending on what is needed to keep students productively engaged in pursuit of a learning outcome. Students with little experience in conducting scientific inquiries will probably require more structure. As students mature and gain experience with inquiry, they will become adept at clarifying good questions, designing investigations to test ideas, interpreting data, and forming explanations based on data. With such students, the teacher still should monitor by observation, ask questions for clarification, and make suggestions when needed. Often, teachers begin the school year providing considerable structure and then gradually provide more opportunities for student-centered investigations. The type and amount of structure can vary depending on what is needed to keep students productively engaged in pursuit of a learning outcome. Students with little experience in conducting scientific inquiries will probably require more structure.

To have productive experiences, inquiry requires considerable planning and organization on the part of both teachers and students. Teachers need to create systems for organization and management of materials and guidelines for student use of materials and conversation. Students need to learn how to work with materials in an organized fashion, communicate their ideas with one another, listen to each other's ideas with respect, and accept responsibility for their own learning. In addition, it always is helpful when students know what is expected of them in terms of behavior and performance.

Author: Inquiry is often viewed as being only of benefit for high achieving students. To what extent is inquiry useful for all students?

BC: Inquiry is appropriate for all students. It is the responsibility of the science teacher to develop inquiry-based lessons that both foster and promote students' curiosity and excitement about the word around them regardless of their abilities. It is the role of the teacher to uncover and explore the most effective instructional techniques to do so.

SECTION:

C

OTHER WAYS OF TEACHING INQUIRY

11

HOW TO INFUSE INQUIRY INTO NON-INQUIRY ACTIVITIES

The most exciting phrase to hear in science, the one that heralds new discoveries, is not Eureka! (I found it!) but rather, "hmm.... that's funny...

Isaac Asinov

In the previous chapters we concentrated on describing the features an inquiry-based science lesson contains and methods you can use to teach these features. However, you might have a non-inquiry experimental protocol in front of you and still be unclear about how exactly to change it to make it more open. In this chapter we show you some of the steps involved in making experiments more open. There are a number of reasons why it is useful for you to learn how to do this.

Although inquiry-based science has been widely promoted by science educators for a number of years, many of the support materials available to teachers remains firmly based on traditional teaching methods. Curriculum materials, school textbooks, and experimental protocols still overwhelmingly offer only non-inquiry experiments, activities and exercises. It is therefore useful for you to be able to convert lesson material you already have to make it more open and more inquiry like.

It is unrealistic to expect students who have never seen or worked in an inquiry-based way to be able use this technique successfully if given a fully open inquiry-based activity. Students should be exposed to inquiry slowly and in a gradual way. You need to be able to add inquiry features to experiments gradually so that students can learn what is expected from them and to become accustomed to inquiry-based learning.

You may not want to teach a particular topic entirely in an inquiry-based way, but may still want to integrate some of the features of inquiry-based science in order to make the experiment or activity more open and more interesting for students.

Seeing the steps involved in changing a traditional activity into a more open inquiry-based one helps you to better understand the ideas and principles behind inquiry-based science and therefore be better able to teach in this way.

Removing the scaffolding

The easiest first step to making an exercise more inquiry-based is to modify who decides how the results of an experiment are communicated (Colburn 2000). In non-inquiry experiments students are often told how to record their results, for example by being given a table to complete or being asked to draw a graph. The first and easiest step in making the experiment more inquiry-based is to change this so that the student decides how to communicate their results. Remove the template data table, and ask the students to decide on a way to present the data.

When the students have become used to doing this, you can go a step further and can consider changing the experimental method or procedure. Colburn (2000) recommends removing parts of the method, for example the measurements to be used, and letting students decide how much of substances to use. Later when students are more accustomed to working in a more open way the method can be removed altogether.

Later you can add other features of an inquiry lesson as is required. The important point is that changes are made gradually, and that students have chance to get used to working in an inquiry-based way. Although students might struggle initially given time they will adapt well and will be able to successfully do full inquiry exercises.

An Example: photosynthesis in pondweed

To help show you how an experiment can be adapted and made more inquiry like an example is shown below which uses a typical school experiment. This is the experiment that looks at which factors affect photosynthesis in pondweed (*Elodea canadensis*). This is a very common experiment, which you will almost certainly have seen or done at some time or other during your school career or while training to become a teacher. First we show you the non-inquiry experiment, and then go through the steps involved in making it more inquiry like, until finally an inquiry-like version of the experiment is shown with all the alterations added.

Traditional exercise;
The rate of photosynthesis of pondweed increases as the light intensity increases

Introduction
Photosynthesis is the process by which plants turn the suns energy into food. In photosynthesis plants use the suns energy along with water and carbon dioxide to make sugar, water and oxygen. The rate of photosynthesis is limited by a number of things including the temperature, light intensity and carbon dioxide level. In this practical we will see that as the light intensity increases the rate of photosynthesis increases.

Method
1) Collect a sprig of pondweed that has been cut off at one end.
2) Place the sprig of pondweed in a beaker of water so that the cut end is well under water but so that the cut end is still visible.
3) Place a bright lamp so that it is shining on the pondweed at 10, 20 and 30 cm away from the pondweed. Count the number of bubbles produced by the cut end of the pondweed in 5 minutes at each distance.

Results
Place your results in the following table and on the following graph;

Distance of lamp	Number of bubbles produced
10cm	
20cm	
30cm	

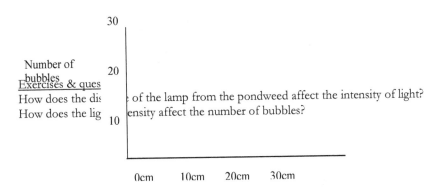

Number of bubbles

Exercises & ques
How does the dis   of the lamp from the pondweed affect the intensity of light?
How does the lig   ensity affect the number of bubbles?

Distance of lamp from pondweed

115

Steps to making the exercise more inquiry like

<u>Discover what prior knowledge students have</u>
Before you can teach something you need to know what your students already know, so why not ask them? Remove the information at the beginning of the exercise and probe your student's knowledge.

Instead of:
Photosynthesis is the process by which plants turn the sun's energy into food. In photosynthesis plants use the energy from the sun along with water and carbon dioxide to make a sugar, water and oxygen. The rate of photosynthesis is limited by a number of things including the temperature, light intensity and carbon dioxide level. In this practical we will see that as the light intensity increases the rate of photosynthesis increases.

Use:
What do you know about how plants make food using the suns energy? Make a list with your partner.

<u>Do not tell the students what they should find</u>
By telling the students what they should find the experiment just becomes a confirmation exercise. Let the students discover something instead. Try to get students to think what could happen instead. By getting students to predict they will be thinking about what they are about to do.

Instead of:
*In pondweed the rate of photosynthesis increases as the light intensity increases **and** in this practical we will see that as the light intensity increases the rate of photosynthesis increases.*

Use:
Which of these graphs do you believe is correct? The light intensity is on the x axis and the number of bubbles produced on the y axis.

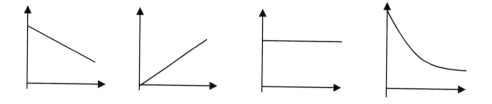

<u>Remove the table or area in which the results are collected</u>
Students need to understand why they are collecting data. They need to understand the meaning and value of the data they collect. If students have to design their own ways of collecting and analyzing data they will hopefully understand which data are important.

Instead of:

Results
Place your results in the following table;

Distance of lamp	Number of bubbles produced
10cm	
20cm	
30cm	

Use:
Decide which results to collect and how to record them.

Remove or modify the instructions
In a traditional lab there is usually a step-by-step list of instructions. Normally listed or numbered. Students simply have to follow these to do the experiment. At first you could remove specific instructions and make them more open to interpretation. Later you can remove them altogether and let the students decide what to do.

Instead of:

Method
  1) *Collect a 10 to 15 cm long sprig of pondweed that has been cut off at one end.*
  2) *Take a full beaker of water. Place the sprig of pondweed in the beaker so that the cut end is well under water.*
  3) *Place a bright lamp so that it is shining on the pondweed at 10, 20 and 30 cm away from the pondweed. Count the number of bubbles produced by the cut end of the pondweed in 5 minutes at each distance.*

Use:

Collect a small sprig of pondweed that has been cut off at one end. Place it underwater so that bubbles can be seen coming from the cut end. Shine a lamp on the pondweed sprig. See what effect altering the distance of the lamp from the pondweed has on the amount of gas the pondweed produces.

Or use:
Using the available equipment conduct an experiment to find how the distance of a lamp from a sprig of pondweed affects the rate at which it produces gas bubbles. Decide on the method to use before you begin.

Change the questions at the end of the practical
The questions at the end of the practical are often low level knowledge or comprehension based questions. These do not force the students to think, but instead to recall knowledge. Use higher-level questions. Try to get students to think of different things they could experiment, or to

generate new questions. What do you believe the experiment shows? What ideas can you add? How would you investigate…?

Instead of:
- *How does the distance of the lamp from the pondweed affect the intensity of light?*
- *What happens when the intensity of light is increased?*

Use:

- The bubbles are produced because the pondweed is photosynthesizing. Photosynthesis is the process in which plants make energy from the sun's energy. During this process they take in carbon dioxide and give out oxygen. Why do you think the number of bubbles the pondweed produces increases when the light is closer to the pondweed?

- Many things could affect the rate at which the pondweed produces bubbles, for example the amount of CO_2 or the temperature. How could you investigate the effect of these factors, and others, on the photosynthesis of pondweed?

Discuss limitations
Talk about the problems with the experiment and how it could be made better.

Use questions like:
What problems can you see with the experiment? What could you do about these problems?

How could the size of the bubbles affect the results? Could light from other sources affect the results?

Provide students with opportunities to communicate their results to others
This allows students to compare ideas with others and to generate more ideas of their own.

Use:
At the end of the experiment one person from each group will stand up and tell the class what results their group found.

Bubble production in pondweed (Inquiry like)

Introduction

Work in groups of 3 to complete the following tasks. Later you will discuss you r results with the whole class.

What do you know about how plants make food using the sun's energy? Make a list with your partner.

Which of the following graphs do you think is correct? (light intensity is on the x axis and the number of bubbles produced is on the y axis.

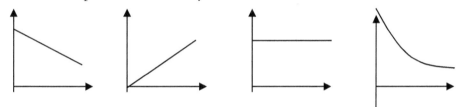

Or do you think something else is correct? If so draw your own graph.

How could you find out which one is correct? Think of some ideas in your group and write them down.

Method

Using the available equipment you shall conduct an experiment to find how light affects the number of bubbles produced in the pondweed.

Decide on the method to use before you begin. Write down your ideas and plans and then have them checked by your teacher.

Decide which results to collect and how to record them. Why do you think this is a good way to collect and record your results? Write down your reasons.

At the end of the experiment one person from each group will stand up and tell the class what results their group found. How will you organize this presentation? What will you include, why?

Problems

Answer these questions after giving your group presentation.
What problems can you see with the experiment? What could you do about these problems?

How could the size of the bubbles affect the results?

Could light from other sources affect the results?

Questions for homework

Why do you think the number of bubbles the pondweed produces increases when the light is closer to the pondweed?

Will the number of bubbles produced always increase as the intensity of light increases? Discuss.

Many things could affect the rate at which the pondweed produces bubbles, for example the amount of CO^2 or the temperature. How could you investigate the effect of these factors, and others, on the photosynthesis of pondweed?

LEARNING CYCLES

Research is what I'm doing when I don't know what I'm doing.

Werner von Braun

The process of learning has been modeled as a continuous cycle by a number of different authors in a number of different forms. These methods of representing learning in a cyclical manner are commonly known as 'Learning Cycles.' They are useful to science educators because they break the process of learning down into discrete stages.

For learning to occur learners need to successfully complete each stage before progressing to the next one. Only when the learner has had the opportunity to complete each and every stage is learning successful. The stages are connected together in a cyclical pattern, and this means that learning is a continual process to which there is no end. A core feature of Learning Cycles is that they rely on children gaining concrete experiences. This means they support constructivist and inquiry methods of teaching.

The work of Kurt Lewin (1942) is commonly acknowledged as being the inspiration behind learning cycles, although the ideas of a number of other pedagogic researchers such as John Dewey also played a role in their development. Many of the ideas that provide a foundation for Learning Cycles can be found in Lewins' book 'Field Theory and Learning.'

Karplus and Their Learning Cycle:

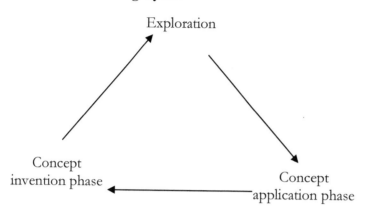

As can be seen this method bears similarities with the discovery learning method of teaching. Whereas in discovery learning students simply have the opportunity to discover new ideas through active hands-on learning, the learning cycle takes this further and encourages the formation of explanations by the students and then a reinforcement of these ideas through the use of a new activity.

A good example of how this learning cycle could be used in an actual lesson is with the teaching of motion. Students could be given marbles and instructed to study how they role, hit each other, and the speeds they travel at. This would follow the first step of the cycle. Next the teacher would provide the students with the principles and ideas that influence the balls, in the Concept Invention Phase. Lastly the students could be given some task to perform and use these newly discovered ideas and their labels, for example by writing a description of how balls roll and hit against each other.

The Kolb learning cycle

David Kolb (1984) developed a different version of the learning cycle, this time made up of 4 stages. These were:
1. Concrete experience: in which the learner develops an experience by being actively engaged in some task.
2. Reflection: this is where the learner reviews what happened while they were doing the task. The learner has time to think about what they did.
3. Abstract Conceptualization: in this stage the learner tries to understand and make sense of what happened in the previous two stages. The learner tries to fit what they saw on to their pre-existing ideas.
4. Active experimentation: the learner uses the new ideas to conduct experiments. Predictions are made on what will happen, based on what happened previously and the learners new ideas. This stage naturally blends back into concrete experience.

There are a number of implications of the Kolb Learning Cycle. For learning to be successful a learner has to complete each step. If one stage is left out or neglected, then learning will be hampered. Teachers therefore need to consider how they can effectively teach all steps to make their teaching most effective.

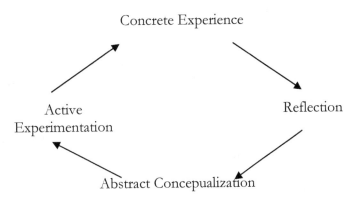

It is thought that each stage is best suited to different types of individuals (Honey and Mumford 1982). The concrete experience stage is best suited to an 'activist' person, someone who prefers dong and experimenting. The 'reflector' someone who observes and then thinks about what they have seen is best at the reflective observation phase. A 'theorist' is best at abstract conceptualization, and a 'pragmatist' is able to do active experimentation best. This means that teachers have to make minor adjustments to how they teach in order to suit the type of individual they are teaching to allow them to progress to the next stage.

The Kolb model makes clear that there are two types of knowledge. During the concrete experience stage knowledge is generated by hands-on personal experience. The knowledge gained in this way is 'knowledge by acquaintance'. The learner knows something because they have experienced it for themselves. During the abstract conceptualization stage knowledge is gained through comprehension and understanding and not through direct experience. Ideas are known but have not been gained through self-discovery.

What could each stage of Kolb's model involve?:
1. Concrete Experience: Discovery Learning, a team task or activity.
2. Reflective observation: Group Brainstorming, question and answer session, discussion.
3. Abstract Conceptualization: personal interpretation, individual question answering, individual brainstorming.
4. Active Experimentation: Group planning and experimentation.

Bybee's 5E learning cycle

The 5E Learning Cycle was developed for the BSCS by Roger Bybee (BSCS, 1970). This uses the framework already established in previous learning cycles, but makes them more applicable and useable for inquiry-based situations. The 5E learning cycle is made up of 5 stages. 3 of these, explore, explain and elaborate are present in the previously mentioned learning cycles under different names, but two more stages are added, the engage and the evaluation stages to enhance the inquiry qualities of the lesson.

- **Engage:** In the engage stage the student's interest is awoken, and students are forced to find a problem or are given a problem. During this stage the teacher uses questioning to probe students prior knowledge and conceptions.
- **Exploration**: This is where students are allowed to do some hands-on practical work. This can be in the form of discovery learning, with the students being allowed to work without direction to form their own ideas. The idea is that students try to answer questions or solve problems they formed or were given by the teacher in the engage stage. The teacher simply allows students to explore on their own.
- **Explanation**: In this stage the teacher helps the students understand what they found out in the explore stage. The teacher can do this by asking questions that forces students to think about what they saw or did, or the teacher can introduce concepts, ideas or labels.
- **Elaboration**: In the elaboration phase the knowledge they obtained in the explanation stage is built upon. The students get to use their new skills on a new task or activity. It is a kind of reinforcement of the ideas learnt. This can be done through an inquiry-based experiment.
- **Evaluation**: The evaluation stage is used by the teacher to assess the progress the students have made. This can take the form of traditional assessment or more modern ideas.

Rather confusingly, although the 5E model is an example of a learning cycle, it is mostly portrayed in a linear fashion, with each step numbered 1 to 5 or simply listed. However, the 5E model still works in a circular fashion, learners who reach the evaluate stage, should generate new questions which allow them to move again to the engage stage.

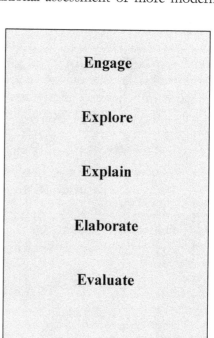

‚The learning cycle' and inquiry-based science

The development of the learning cycles has a number of implications for inquiry-based science teaching. As mentioned the Learning Cycles provide a template for learning that is based on constructivist ideas, and because similar ideas are utilized in inquiry-based science, both methods are complimentary. Inquiry-based science lessons can be planned and designed using the idea of learning cycles as a structure and as the 'backbone' of the lesson. A number of authors have developed inquiry-based lessons based on Learning Cycles. For example *Teaching Science through Inquiry* by Carin et al. (2005) provides a large number of examples of science lessons all utilizing this system. The 5E learning cycle is the one most commonly used and seems to be the most suitable for use in inquiry contexts.

Using learning cycles to structure inquiry-based lessons

The learning cycles are ideal to help structure lessons that contain inquiry-based elements. Teachers often would like to teach using an inquiry-based practical or experiment, but are unsure as to how to plan lessons around this, or how to begin and end the lesson. The Learning Cycle provides a structure that embeds the inquiry exercise into the lesson, in a way that supports students in their use of inquiry. As mentioned above in the 5E Learning Cycle inquiry-based exercises can be used in exploration or the elaboration phases of the lesson. The other phases of the lesson help introduce the topic, or allow the teacher to provide explanations to the students.

Advantages of using learning cycles

There are a number of advantages to using Learning Cycles to teach inquiry:

Flexibility: Learning Cycles allow teachers a certain amount of flexibility. Teachers can adapt phases to their own needs, and teach them in the way they feel best with. Phases can be shortened or lengthened as required. Teachers can cut down the standard 5E learning cycle to a 3 stage cycle with only the explore, explain, elaborate phases if they wish. As mentioned inquiry-based exercises can be used either in the explore or the elaborate phases. Despite this flexibility the stages of the learning cycles still provide a structure for the lesson.

Learning over several lessons: Learning Cycles are useful when wishing to teach a topic over a number of lessons. The teacher can plan which phases to teach in which lessons. For example in the first lesson he or she might start with the engage and explore phases, for example in a lesson about 'bridges', the teacher might introduce the topic and then allow students to make bridges using straws, paper and play dough. In the second lesson the teacher would teach the explain phase, and simply give a standard lecture about different designs of bridges and why they vary in strength. In the third lesson the elaborate and evaluate phases would be used, for example the students could be given the challenge to design and build the strongest bridge possible in an inquiry-based way.

The Teaching of Content: One reason teachers are suspicious of inquiry-based learning is that they feel it does not allow them the opportunity to teach science content or to provide explanations to students. The Learning Cycle provides a section, the explain phase, which is dedicated to the acquisition of content knowledge and in which teachers can offer explanations. The explain phase does not simply have to involve lecturing of students, it can take the form of a discussion, or a question and answer session, allowing students to explain and think about the things they discovered in the explore phase and thus to build their own knowledge.

The Teaching of Scientific Methods: One problem with inquiry-based learning is that it is difficult to teach specific scientific methods. Think about the Benedict's test for sugar, this is a difficult procedure involving a number of steps that have to be done correctly. How could you teach students to do a Benedict's test in an inquiry way? They first have to learn to use the procedure before they can use it in an inquiry investigation. The 5E Learning Cycle allows for the teaching of scientific techniques and methods, and then their use in inquiry. For example in the explore stage, students could do a standard confirmation style Benedict's experiment testing for sugar, in order to simply learn how to do the technique. Later in the elaborate phase, students could have the opportunity to conduct a much more open inquiry activity, in which they design an experiment to find out if different cola's contain different amount of sugars. In such a way students learn both a technique, and then how to use it in an inquiry way.

CONSTRUCTING EXTENDED INQUIRY PROJECTS

We haven't the money, so we've got to think.

Ernest Rutherford

Teachers tend to prefer to give their students practical exercises that can be fitted into a single lesson. This is mainly because it is easier to plan and organize lessons on a lesson-by-lesson basis. Experiments that can be completed and 'tidied away' within a single hour are self contained and discrete. There is always the danger that your students will forget what they were doing in previous lessons if experiments or studies are carried over, or that the structure of the topic being taught gets lost and then time gets wasted.

There are often content rich curricula to follow, and this means you have to try to move from one topic to the next in quick succession in order to fit everything into the school year. Experiments need to be done quickly to allow you to 'move on.' This means extended work gets neglected.

Despite these pressures you should try to include some extended activities or experiments in science classes during the school year. There are a number of advantages to doing work over several lessons, weeks or even months. Students learn that sometimes it takes time to do experiments. Science is not always 'instant'. Good results are obtained only with the exertion of time and effort. Extended projects allow students to develop their ideas and fully think about what they are doing. Often with time students' perspectives change. In some science topics such as ecology and meteorology time is an important factor and by nature these subjects rely on time.

Inquiry-based techniques offer a good way for you to introduce experiments that need a longer period of time than a single lesson. Here are some examples of inquiry-based exercises that you can teach over a longer time span than the normal single lesson.

What earthworms do

Teaching aims

The aim of this teaching unit is to show students:
- The role of earthworms in the ecosystem.
- How earthworms act as decomposers of waste and tillers of the soil.
- How to design experiments.

Introduction

A good way to introduce this topic is to ask students to imagine that they heard the news that life had been found on mars. Little animals that lived in burrows beneath the surface had been discovered. But as of yet there are no pictures. What do you think the newly discovered animals look like? What features do you think they possess? How would it move? What would it eat?

What would the Martian-underground-living-animal be like?
- It would be thin and round so that it could crawl into small spaces easily.
- It would have something like claws, so that it could dig into the ground.
- It would be slimy so that it could squeeze easier through gaps.
- It could see in the dark.
- It would suck things from the surface to eat.

Next you could ask the students to draw what they think the Martian animal looks like, and to label its main features. Once the students have done this they should be asked to compare their animals with what an earthworm is like. Ask them to use the Internet, textbooks, or school models to find out what an earthworm is like in structure and then to compare it to the imagined animals.

In what ways are earthworms similar to your Martian animals? In which ways are they different?

Generating a question to investigate

The teacher could ask the students which things affect how earthworms work at decomposing matter. When would earthworms be slow at decomposing things and when quick? The teacher could use these statements to prompt the following questions from the students.

The obvious questions for this exercise are:
- What effect does temperature have on earthworm activity?
- Do earthworms work better in dry or wet soils?
- How does the number of worms affect the speed of decomposition?
- How long does it take different amounts of leaf litter to be decomposed?

Planning an experiment

The class could be split into groups, each group looking at one specific question. Each group could be asked to provide the following:

- The question they are going to answer.
- A hypothesis about the question.
- A list of variables in the experiment, and which ones they will alter and which one they will keep the same.
- A design for how they could conduct the experiment.

Conducting the experiment

There are a number of ways the students could do this. Students should decide for themselves how to set up the experiment. Here is only a suggestion.

Worm Density: Plastic plant pots, of 10 to 15 cm in diameter, could be filled with earth. The soil would be kept equally damp in each plant pot. In each pot grass mower clippings, or leaves or biodegradable household garbage could be added. The same amount should be added to each pot. A layer of between 1 and 5 cm is usually adequate. I suggest a large cup full. In one pot no worms would be added, in one pot 10 worms should be added, in the next 20, and the next 50. The pots should then be left in a cool shady place. Each few days the depths of the level of garbage or clippings are be measured and compared with the starting level. Worms can normally be bought from fishing supply shops.

Temperature: Worms would be added to several plastic pots as above, the pots would be placed in different locations with different temperatures. For example one pot could be put in a warm sunny spot and one in a cold area. The depth of biodegradable waste would be recorded each few days.

Humidity: Worms should be placed in plant pots that have been wet with different amounts of water. Then the pots should be placed somewhere close together and the depth of biodegradable household waste remaining recorded regularly.

Students should be prompted to record results but should decide themselves what exactly to record and how to record it. If the students want to extend their investigations to investigate other factors then they should be allowed to.

Communicating the results

After some weeks the students should be able to communicate their findings to the class. They could do this by making a poster showing how they set up the experiment and what they found. They could present their poster to the class.

Connecting the experiment with everyday life

To extend the project the students could design possible containers to decompose household waste as quickly as possible. They could use the Internet to search for ways in which waste is composted and how waste products are dealt with. They could decide whether there are better ways for dealing with waste and if so what they could be. They could also do research onto other animals or microbes that help to break down waste and what factors affect the speed they break waste down at.

Teacher Experience

Dr. Norman Budnitz, a member of the Center for Inquiry-Based Learning (CIBL) at Duke University and a former middle and high school teacher describes one extended inquiry-based science project he has taught.

Author: Have you every used inquiry in a long-term project?
NB: I had a middle school class in which we raised mosquitoes by collecting leaf litter from a stream edge. We watched the larvae after they hatched, and built cages for the adults. There was lots of inquiry, because the students kept generating lots of questions and then had to figure out where to find the answers.

Author: What advantages did you see of using inquiry over a longer time span?
NB: Students get to 'see,' not just 'look.' Students have to really work on something. They can't just get a quick answer and move on. The process of chewing on a topic for a while really helps to solidify learning.

Author: What did the students learn that would not have been possible in a single lesson?
NB: The mosquitoes were real. They were motionless. They wriggled. They flew. They hummed. Sometimes they just did nothing for very long periods of time. So the students learned that real animals do real things at their own pace.

Author: Were there any management problems? For example with group members missing important lessons due to illness, students forgetting what they had done, or getting bored with the projects? How did you combat these problems?
NB: Since students worked collaboratively, there was generally someone to make the observations when someone else might have been absent. There was always someone to take responsibility for what needed to be done. And the collaboration required communication about what might have been missed.

Boredom is real and a fact of life. That was actually an important part of the activity. In general, when the critters weren't active, there were other tasks that could be done. For example, if the larvae weren't active, there was cage-designing or building to do. Or there was 'book learning' to do, like looking up things in the encyclopedia to learn about diseases. The trick for me as a teacher was to have something up my sleeve whenever things dragged too much.

Author: What did your students find out? What did they learn?

NB: They observed the complete life cycle of mosquitoes. They also learned a lot about the impact of mosquitoes on humans and other organisms.

Author: How did what the students did mirror real science? Why is its easy to mirror real science in longer term projects?
This WAS real science in the sense of making long-term observations to learn about the life cycle of a particular organism. It was also real science in that things didn't always work out as expected. Wrigglers died. Adults escaped. Students had to grapple with these occurrences and try to fix things in order to get better results.

Science is not something that has one right answer that can be found in 45 minutes. Science is process and it takes time. This is not to say that all science can be taught using long-term inquiry projects. Students can't be expected to come up with evolutionary theories or Newtonian mechanics on their own. Some things are best taught via textbooks and/or lectures. But the 'experience' of science makes those other modes much more interesting and real.

What factors affect germination in bean seeds?

Germination and the factors that affect germination are themes often seen in biology curricula. In this exercise students get to study some of the factors that affect germination by designing and conducting their own experiment. The experiment is embedded within an inquiry-based context. Some weeks are needed for the successful completion of the experiment.

Lesson aims

The aim of this practical exercise is to help students understand:
- The process of germination.
- The structure of seeds.
- The factors that initiate the process of germination.

Introduction

To introduce the topic of germination the teacher could do a number of things:
- Show the class a jam jar with a germinated bean seed in it, and then prompt the class to think about what happened to the seed and why. What has happened to the seed? Why? How could you stop this happening? What makes the seed germinate?

- Give the students a germinated and a not germinated bean seed, and ask them to draw them and find the differences between the two. The students could open the bean seeds and draw the differences they see. The teacher would ask questions about what the students draw. What differences do you see? What do you think the different parts of the seed do? Where do you think the root and the stem grow from?

- Show the class growing plants and seeds of different heights. Ask them to compare the seeds and plants and to say what differences they see. Ask the students: How long does it take seeds to begin to grow? What happens when seeds begin to grow? What happens inside the seeds when it grows?

Generating questions and a hypothesis

The best way to get students to generate questions is to ask them which factors they think affect or are needed for germination, write these ideas on the blackboard, and then turn them into a question.

Temperature affects germination.
Does temperature affect germination?

Light affects germination.
Does the amount of light affect germination?

Water is needed for germination.
Is water needed for germination?

The size of the seed affects germination.
Does the size of the seed affect germination?

There are many possible factors that affect seed growth. If the students have problems finding these factors then help them, this is the most difficult part of inquiry-based science. Split the class into groups and ask each group to investigate one factor. Ask each group to take one question, make a hypothesis from it, and then design an experiment to find out if it affects germination. Consider using some of the prompt sheets shown in earlier chapters to help students do this.

You can tell the students they will be able to use jam-jars in which to grow the seeds in. A piece of thick card can be rolled up and placed into the jam-jar so that it stands upright. Use a stapler to place staples on the card, around which bean seeds can be suspended. The jam-jars can then be filled with a little water. When the card becomes wet the seed will start to germinate.

Designing an experiment

Students may need help to design an experiment themselves. They need to consider which variables are present and how to control them. Possible variables include temperature, the amount of water and the amount of light. The students need to ensure that they keep all the variables apart from the one they are studying constant. The group studying if light affects germination could put one germination chamber in a dark cupboard and another on a light windowsill. The group looking at temperature could put one germination chamber in a fridge and another in a warm room. Those studying water cold make one chamber without water and another with plentiful water.

One way to help the students plan their experiments is to give them a planning sheet, as shown previously in this book. Or you can simply go around each group asking them suitable questions to see if they understand what they are doing.

Conducting the experiment

Next students should make their germination chambers to test their ideas. The experiment will take some weeks to work effectively. The bean seeds will need time to germinate. The experiment should be left, but you should monitor the germination chambers carefully and continue the lesson when you think it is appropriate.

Interpreting the results

Once the seeds have begun germinating the teacher should get students to look at their experiments and decide what affects their factor had on germination. Did all our seeds germinate? If not why not? Does this prove or disprove our hypothesis? You should ask the students questions such as these to force them to think about the results they have and why they obtained them. When each group has looked at their results and decided what they mean, each group should design a poster showing how they conducted their experiment and what the results mean. At the end of the lesson the teacher can summarize the main points they have found. At this stage the teacher could ask the students questions to make the experiment more relevant to the lives of the students and to reinforce their knowledge.

Why are the results you found important for people like farmers? What can farmers do to help seeds grow successfully? If you want to grow flowers from seed at home where will you put them and what will you do to them?

How could the experiment we did be improved? What could we make better? Could we have tested any other factors? How?

Making a mini-ecosystem

There are various versions of this inquiry-based experiment of getting students to build their own ecosystem using pondweed and aquatic invertebrates (Thomas et al 2005, TERC 1998).

Lesson aims

The aims of the lesson is to show students:
- External energy is needed for an ecosystem to function.
- That in an ecosystem there is a cycling of nutrients.
- There is a connection between living things in an ecosystem.

Introduction

In this exercise students will make a mini ecosystem using pondweed and water snails. They must see how long the mini ecosystem lasts for and what changes happen to the ecosystem with time. One way to introduce this topic is to tell the students to imagine a greenhouse that contains some plants and some snails. The greenhouse is a self-contained container in which nothing can get in or out. It is made out of glass, but there are no windows that open and the greenhouse is airtight.

Questions a teacher could ask about this scenario:
- From where does the oxygen in the greenhouse come? (The plants produce oxygen through photosynthesis)

- Who uses up the oxygen in the greenhouse? (Both the snails and the plants breathe oxygen)

- What do the snails eat? (The snails feed on the plants)

- What happens if the number of snails increases? What happens if the number of plants decreases? (It is like a cycle. If the number of snails increases there will be fewer plants, this will mean that some snails will die, and then the plants can recover and increase.)

Ask the students to think about the greenhouse. Explain this is a type of ecosystem. Ask the students how long they think the ecosystem could last?

Generating questions and a hypothesis

The students will now have the opportunity to build their own mini-ecosystems using plastic bottles, pondweed and water snails. Introduce these separate elements to the students and tell them they will be making a mini ecosystem. Before they make their mini ecosystems the students should first think about what things they need to consider if the ecosystem is to work.

How much pondweed is needed? How many water snails should be added? How do you decide on the 'balance' between water snails and pondweed?

Students need to look at the cycle of events that happens in the ecosystem. The pondweed has a dual function, firstly it oxygenates the water meaning the water snails have enough oxygen to breathe, and secondly the pondweed acts as a food source for the water snail. If there are too many water snails they will eat too much and the pondweed will all disappear.

What questions will the students need to know the answer to before beginning to make their ecosystem? Possible questions:

- How much do snails eat? (So you can guess how many snails to add to the ecosystem).

- How much oxygen does pondweed produce? How can you make pondweed photosynthesize quicker? (This is important is deciding where to place the ecosystem, and deciding who much pondweed to add at the beginning).

- How much water needs to be added to the ecosystem? (So that the pondweed and snails have enough to live in).

Planning and conducting an experiment

The practical can run in two different ways from here. Either the students can work in groups to answer one of these questions by designing and conducting an experiment, and then use their answer to help them design their ecosystem. Or the students can go directly to making their own ecosystem, and can simply consider these questions in how they build their ecosystem.

If students conduct experiments to answer these questions they will have to design suitable experiments. To study how much snails eat students could place a certain weight of pondweed in a container with snails and after 2 or 3 days, reweigh the pondweed to see how much has been eaten per snail. To study the rate of photosynthesis in pondweed is fairly simple and has already been explained in this book. To test how much water is needed in the ecosystems students can test different bottles with different amounts of water and simply see in which ones pondweed and the snails survives.

Making the ecosystems

Once students have either conducted their experiments, or have considered the above questions they can go onto making their ecosystems. They should take into full consideration the results of their experiments and the questions above when making their ecosystems. Students need to decide how much pondweed to add, how much water, and how many snails. They should be able to justify why they add these amounts to their ecosystem. Students also need to decide what size or type of bottle to use, and where they will place their ecosystem when it is finished.

Once the students have finished their ecosystems they should be left in a suitable place. Students can observe the ecosystems on a regular basis, and maybe record what is happening over time. It is also a good idea to get students to predict how long the ecosystems will last at the beginning of the exercise, and then to get them to see if they are right or not. The ecosystems will probably last a lot longer than the students thought. They can often last many months before finally 'dying' and stopping to be a functioning ecosystem.

OTHER WAYS OF CONDUCTING SCIENCE

The airplane stays up because it doesn't have the time to fall.

Orville Wright

The examples of inquiry-based science investigations used so far in this book have mostly been of experiments. If you look back at chapter 2, you will see that experimentation is only one way of doing science. Documentation, inventing, product testing and trial and error are also valid ways of doing science. In this section some of these others methods of conducting science are discussed and examples of how to integrate them into an inquiry-based lesson are given.

Documentation

Documentation is the making of observations and the taking of data over a long period of time. Many teachers prefer practical work to last a single period, but some investigations need substantially more time. Inquiry-based science is especially well suited to longer term projects because it provides a framework or structure in which lessons can be taught. Often practical work that is conducted over some weeks loses direction.

There are a number of good examples of longer-term projects using documentation that students can do within an inquiry framework. A commonly given example is that students could keep a moon diary (Koch 2000, Carin et al. 2005), each night recording what phase the moon is in. To be done properly this needs to be done for at least 4 weeks, so that all phases of the moon are seen and patterns can begin to be recognized. Other examples include the recording of weather over the seasons, or measuring the speed at which plants grow. For these projects to be considered as authentic inquiry, it is essential that they are based on some scientific question, and that they lead to the collection of evidence and the formulation of explanations on the part of the students.

An example of documenting: A moon diary

A good example of a way to use documenting in a science lesson is to study the phases of the moon (Carin, 2005). Students were given the task of keeping a 'moon diary' over the period of 4 weeks. Students were asked to observe the moon each evening and to record what they saw. The students were asked to record the position of the moon, its size, and its shape. They were asked to draw pictures of the moon through its different phases. Once students had had the chance to record the stages of the moon through a whole cycle they were taught about the moons phases.

Making models

Making models is an important scientific activity. Many models are mathematical, and help scientists to answer questions, predict what will happen in the future and how things will change over time. For example there are complex mathematical models that show how populations change over time. Today many of these models are computer based.

Other models are physical and help the scientist to visualize something that otherwise cannot be seen or touched or manipulated. For example the structure of DNA is often represented as a model of a ladder like double helix. The supports of the ladders are the sugar phosphate parts of DNA, while the rungs of the ladder are the nucleotide bases. This helps us to understand the structure of DNA and how it works much better than if all the chemical structures were listed in detail exactly as they are. Another example would be a model showing how the lungs work, using a rubber glove that inflates and deflates. It is impossible for students to see how a lung works in a real human body, so using a model is the best way.

It is important to remember that the actual making of a model is not the purpose of the lesson. A model should be made to allow some question to be answered or some problem to be solved. Making a model is a scientific activity, but only when the model is actually used to solve a problem are you working in a scientific way.

Product testing

Many scientists work on testing products. Most of the objects we use every day need to be tested to ensure they are safe and effective. The most well known example of this is the tests that cars have to undergo to ensure they are safe. Scientists recreate crashes using crash car dummies to see what would happen to the occupants in a crash. The results obtained from this research helps designers to make cars that are even safer in the future. Different makes of cars are tested, and this means customers can see which types of car are the safest and this might influence which one they buy.

Another well-known example of product testing is often seen on adverts for washing powder. These adverts often show scientists in white lab coats testing different brands of washing powder to show how effective they are on different stains. Many companies employ scientists to find out whether their product is better than the competitors. For example a large chocolate company might employ researchers to test which brands of chocolate are customers favorite and why.

138

An example of model making: The solar system

One example of using models in an inquiry-based way can be seen with an example with the solar system. Students were asked to use different types of fruit to represent the planets and then to scale the distances between the planets so that the 'model' could be made on the playing field outside the classroom.

Students were allowed to use books or the Internet to find out information about the size of the planets and the distances between them. They first had to decide which fruits should represent which planets, for example with larger fruits like grapefruits representing the larger planets like Jupiter. Secondly they had to scale down the distances between the planets so that it could be fitted onto the playing field. The teacher helped them do this.

Once they had worked out these things, the whole class went outside with the fruits and a meter stick. Each 'planet' was given to a student who had to hold it. The students took turns measuring out the correct distances between the planets. When the 'model' was complete, the students with the fruit planets were instructed to move in 'orbits' like how the real planets would. The teacher used the model to explain to the students why planets further away form the sun longer to orbit the sun than those closer to it.

An example of product testing: Which chocolate biscuit is the best?

Students can be asked to find out which type or brand of chocolate biscuit is the best. They could do this in various ways. They could design and make a questionnaire that students could answer; the results could then be used to decide which brand of chocolate biscuit is the best. Students could conduct taste tests, and ask students to decide which biscuits taste the best. Students could make a checklist with features they most like about chocolate biscuits and then rate each brand. At the end of the lesson each group could explain which brand they think is the best and why.

Inventing

One of the main advantages of inventing is that students think it is fun! Another advantage is that when students are inventing or designing something they use the steps of inquiry automatically. Although students might not state that they have a problem, a question, a hypothesis, and a plan, etc. while designing and inventing they are using and developing all the steps seen in an inquiry-based lesson.

For example a student trying to design a paper plane which flies well, might think that if the wings are made in a certain way the plane will fly further; he or she then makes the design, tests it, and decides whether he or she was right or not. The student knew what the problem was (How can I get the plane to fly well?), and developed an investigation question and hypothesis (Question; does changing the wing design make it fly better? Hypothesis; Changing the wing design will make it fly better), and then tests the plane and sees whether the hypothesis is correct or not (My plane flew better, my hypothesis is correct).

An example of inventing: Clock candles

One imaginative way to integrate inventing into science is to get students to make clock candles. These are candles that show the time that has elapsed since they started to burn. In order to make clock candles students first have to investigate what factors influence the speed at which candles burn.

Students can be split into groups. First each group has to work out how long it takes candles to burn down a certain distance. Then they have to investigate one of the factors that influence the speed at which candles burn. For example students could investigate how the thickness of the candle influences the speed at which it burns, or its length, or the temperature of the room in which the candle is burning, or what the candle is made of. Students would have to design and conduct an experiment to look at one of these factors.

In the next stage of the lesson the students have to use the results they have collected to produce a working clock candle. They have to decide how to mark candles, at which distances, and how quickly they will burn down. Students could do 'trial runs' to see if there estimates of burning times are correct or not. At the end of the lesson there could be a competition with the teacher lighting all the candles made at the front of the class. The one that is judged to keep time the best is the winner!

There are a large number of possible ideas to get students designing and inventing. Inventing and design lends itself particularly well to physics lessons, where a variety of different things can be built and designed using physics ideas and theories, but can also be used in other disciplines. Some possible ideas for scientific inventions include:

- **Leaves:** Make an identification key for tree leaves.

- **Flowers:** Design and make an identification key for flowers.

- **Train:** Build a levitating train using magnets.

- **Sundial:** Design and make your own sundial.

- **Paper:** Make recycled paper from old.

- **Cell:** Make your own electrochemical cell.

- **A Car:** Design a model car made from wood that is powered by rubber bands.

- **Rockets:** Design a simple rocket. See who's can travel the highest and the furthest.

- **Balloon Popper:** Design and make a machine to automatically pop a balloon.

- **Egg Holder:** Design a holder for an egg that protects it when it is dropped from height.

Inquiry-based competitions

A similar idea to that of getting students to invent things is to use contests or competitions as the basis for inquiry-based lessons. If students feel they have some challenge to complete, they are more motivated and teambuilding within the group is enhanced. Many students find competing with other students fun and interesting. Many of the ideas that can be used for contests help promote problem-solving and analysis skills. Many of the ideas given for possible inventions can be adapted and turned into contests. Who can build the biggest tower? Who can make a rocket that travels furthest? Below are possible ideas and a couple of examples:

- Tower Building: Who can build the tallest tower?

- Paper Plane Making: Who can design and make a paper plane able to fly the longest distance?

- Bridge Building: Who can design a bridge to hold the greatest weight?

- Snail/Woodlice/Worm Racing: Who can make a snail travel the greatest distance in a certain amount of time?

- Compost: Who can turn garden waste into compost in the quickest time possible?

- Plant growing: Who can grow the tallest sunflower? Who can grow the largest marrow?

- Rubber Band Car: Who can design a rubber band powered car that travels the furthest?

Example inquiry-based science lesson
Who can save the egg?

Description

Students always find this activity fun. They are given the task of designing protection for an egg that is going to be thrown out of a third storey window. This is a commonly used method of introducing design into the classroom. We have always found that students come up with ingenious solutions. We allow students to name their eggs and paint faces onto them, thus ensuring a certain amount of empathy with the eggs as they fall!

Materials

We usually provide the following materials:
- A small number of cloth towels
- Paper and card
- Sticky tape
- String

Procedure
1. We ask students to work in groups of 3. Each group is given an egg, which they are expected to name. The task is to design some device to protect their eggs from impact. We later throw the eggs from out of a high window.
2. Students are allowed to use only the materials provided. It is best if the number of cloth towels is limited, otherwise every group simply wraps their egg in a blanket, which is relatively easy and requires little effort.
3. Students are allowed 30 minutes to produce their final design.
4. At the end of the 30 minutes one member from each group goes upstairs to an open window, while all other students go outside and stand in view (not underneath) the open window. The eggs are dropped one by one from the window onto the concrete below. The eggs are then examined. The teams that have managed to prevent damage to their eggs are the winners!

We normally leave the activity at this, but it could be extended in various ways. For example students could design checklists or rubrics to gauge which is the best egg-protecting device. Students could compare how effective different designs are. Most students simply try to cushion the egg by wrapping it in paper. However, we sometimes have students who make parachutes. One group we had rested the egg in a crib of string which were supposed to act as 'shock absorbers.' Unfortunately this did not work, but it would be nice if someone else tried with success.

Example inquiry-based science lesson
Where can you put a nail to make it go rusty?

Lesson Aim

This example of an inquiry-based lesson was developed by Volkmann & Abell (2003). In this lesson students learnt what factors are needed for nails to become rusty. Rust is caused by iron, oxygen, water and an electrolyte coming together. Iron oxide (Fe2O3) is produced.

Materials needed:
- New nails
- Jam jars
- Saltwater, salt, water, weak acid.

Procedure:
1. The lesson was started with the question 'Where can you put a nail to make it go rusty?' being posed. Each student was given a new nail and instructed to take it home and place it somewhere they thought it would rust. Two weeks later the students brought the nails back to school and then had to make a poster explaining where they had placed the nails, why they had placed it where they did, and what they thought rust was.
2. The teacher led a class discussion about rust. The students suggested that air, water, salt and acid cause rust. The teacher asked the students whether they thought one single thing caused rusting or a combination of things.
3. Students were now prompted to design an experiment to test this question. Which variables will you test? What will you change? What will stay the same? What will you observe? What do you predict will happen?
4. Different groups developed and conducted different experiments. For example one group investigated whether saltwater can cause rusting, while another studied whether acid caused rusting. Students designed experiments where nails were placed in jam jars containing different substances or different combinations of substances. These were then probably sealed and then left. The experiments ran for 5 days, with the students making observations on each day.
5. At the end of experimentation the teacher prompted the students to work out what was needed for rusting to occur. The different substances tested were placed on the board and the students were expected to say which combinations caused rusting depending on the results they had collected.

15

TITLE IDEAS FOR INQUIRY LESSONS

Reason and free inquiry are the only effectual agents against error.

Thomas Jefferson

Here are some ideas, which you can use to design your own inquiry-based science lesson. This list is by no means extensive, but is just meant to give you a starting point. The ideas here can be adapted for different types and levels of inquiry. A good way to think of ideas on your own is to use the following sentences as a basis:

What is the effect of: on: ?

How does: affect: ?

Biology

Which factor affects the speed grass grows at most; the amount of moisture, sunlight, or temperature?

Determine if the color of a person's eye affects the vision in light and darkness

What effect do different sounds or types of music have on how plants grow?

The effect of nicotine, air or yeast on the growth of mould.

The growth of seeds given different amounts of fertilizer.

The effect of soap and cleaning products on the growth of mould.

Conduct   an   experiment   to   find   out   the   effect   of   sport   on   learning.

Which factors affect memory and learning?

The effect of cigarettes on plant growth.

Which factors affect plant growth?

Study the effect of salt on plant growth.

The effect on plant growth of different types of artificial light.

What effect does tea have on plant growth?

Study the effect of electricity on plant growth

Can mice see different colors?

Design an experiment to find out if plants move.

How does the ground surface affect the height at which balls bounce to?

Do seeds planted in different orientations grow in different ways?

Do dandelions in a sunny place grow higher than those in shady places?

Which ways of cutting up an onion produces least tears?

Do men and women differ in the sensitiveness of their skin?

Do people from different cultures detect different flavors of food better than others?

How does temperature affect the speed at which bananas ripen?

How does the presence of music affect stamina at exercise?

What effect do different vitamins have on plant growth?

What effect do different types of weed killer have on plants?

How do earthworms react to light, humidity, color, or bird song?

Do mint plants repel insects?

Are there more insects around when the moon is full?

How does the color and background color of text affect how well it can be read?

Do people learn better when exposed to different types of smells?

Does the sight/attractiveness of food affect what we think of its taste?

Does soap or hand cleaning liquid really work at stopping bacterial growth?

An experiment to find out which things attract flies.

Compare the size of a pumpkin with the number of seeds it contains.

Do people weigh different amounts throughout the day?

How can you force a cricket to chirp more?

Does body language show if people lie?

Do areas of different vegetation have different ground temperatures?

Study the effect of coffee on blood pressure.

The effect of sport on blood pressure.

Look at how music affects blood pressure.

How does having breakfast affect school performance?

Which factors affect reaction rates?

Do people remember things they have heard or seen better?

Study how drinking drinks of different temperature affects body temperature.

Which stomach ache tablet works the best at neutralizing acid?

What factors affect photosynthesis in elodea?

Chemistry

What is the effect of ethylene on fruit ripening?

Does temperature affect solubility?

Which factors affect the speed at which food coloring travels through liquid?

Does the temperature at which popcorn is kept affect the number of kernels that do not pop when it is finally cooked?

Does the method used to cook food affect the speed at which it cools?

Conduct an experiment to find the affect of salt on the freezing point of water.

Do soap bubbles last longer on warm or cold days?

Which factors affect the rate of growth of crystals?

How does increasing salinity affect the buoyancy of objects in water?

Test different water resources for acidity.

Does temperature and pH affect salinity of water?

Compare the heat produced by burning different types of rubbish.

Study the effect of different brands of coke on teeth/coins.

Compare how candles burn in beakers of different size.

Which foods release the most energy?

Does recycled paper break down quicker than new paper?

Which factors affect how metal objects rust?

Which factors affect the speed at which crystals form?

Which smoke detectors work the best?

How does temperature affect the elasticity of a rubber band?

Compare different brands of glue and their effectiveness.

How fast will different objects burn in different levels of oxygen?

Compare the effect of different brands and factors of sun cream on protection from the sun.

Is there any difference between white eggshells and brown?

Do different brands of orange juice contain different amounts of vitamin C?

Which brand of washing powder is best at removing stains from clothes?

Are some substances more soluble than others?

Does lemon juice or vinegar act better at dissolving chalk?

Do larger eggs take longer to boil than small eggs?

Do white eggs take longer than brown ones?

How does water temperature affect the speed at which an egg boils?

Does the presence of salt, sugar, pepper, affect the boiling point of water?

Physics

Do more expensive brands of tennis ball bounce better than cheaper ones?

Do older balloons float better or worse than newly filled ones?

Does boiling water in a pan with a lid make it boil quicker or at a lower temperature than water in a pan with no lid?

How does the color of a background affect its absorption of solar insulation?

Which factors affect how a pendulum swings?

How strong are different gauges of nylon fishing line?

What factors affect the bounce of a dropped ball?

How does wetting paper affect its strength?

Does paper thickness affect its strength?

Are rubber bands stronger when it is warmer?

How strong is a toothpick?

Which brand of battery last the longest?

Does temperature affect how fast paint dries?

What affects the strength of electromagnets?

Do different liquids have different surface tension?

What effect does oil have on surface tension?

How does the size of pot and shape of a pot, the amount of water, and the presence of a lid affect the speed at which water boils?

What factors affect the rate of evaporation of water?

How accurate are homemade weather instruments?

How is current in an electric circuit affected by type of conductor, temperature, filament, etc?

Does room temperature affect the lifespan of soap bubbles?

Compare how different metals conduct heat.

Compare metals in density and buoyancy.

What effect does an objects size and mass have on how it sinks in water?

How is the absorbency of a sponge affected by its size?

How is light affected when it passes through water?

How does the number of turns of wire affect electromagnets?

Study the effect of color on heat absorption

Analyze the different heat retention capabilities of straw, sand, paper and cloth.

How do different types of wood burn?

Design a way to measure the speed of sound.

Do different types of fabric dry quicker than others?

Which brands of battery last the longest?

How does the color, thickness, temperature of candle, room temperature etc. effect the speed at which candles burn?

Which keep drinks cooler; cans or bottles?

Study how the size, color, size of neck etc. affects how far balloons travel when the air is let out.

Compare how objects of different size and weight fall to the ground.

Study what affects the distance at which a ball travels when rolled down an incline.

What factors affect the speed at which ice melts?

How does salt affect buoyancy?

How do temperature and humidity affect the life of batteries?

Who can design the electromotor able to produce the most electricity?

Study the effect of water temperature on the buoyancy of a floating object.

Which shape of boat holds the most weight?

How does water temperature affect the speed it takes sugar to dissolve in it?

How does temperature of water affect the speed at which it freezes?

Do energy saving light bulbs produce less light than conventional light bulbs?

What effect does prolonged exposure to sunlight have on paper?

Which substances are the best insulators?

Which type of lawn sprinklers use the least water, or cover the most area with water?

Discover ways to slow down the rate at which ice melts.

Compare how different structures affect how sound travels? Which dampen the sound best?

Does the height from which a ball is dropped affect the height of its bounce?

Which brands of soap make the most long lasting soap bubbles?

What effect does spreading salt on icy roads have?

On which surfaces do balls roll fastest?

Which types of plastic bags are the strongest?

Is wood strength affected by different types of paint covering?

Does putting a spoon in my hot tea make it cool down quicker?

Does the viscosity of oil very with temperature?

16

REFERENCES

Abd-El-Khalick, F., & Lederman, N.G. (2000). Improving science teachers' conceptions of the nature of science: A critical review of the literature. *International journal of science education*, **22,** 665–701.

Andersson, M. (1982). Female choice selects for extreme tail length in a widowbird. *Nature*, **299,** 818-820.

Anderson, R.D. (2002). Reforming Science Teaching: What research says about inquiry. *Journal of Science Teacher Education*, **13,** 1-12.

American Association for the Advancement of Science. (1975). Science: A process approach. *Lexington, MA: Ginn.*

American Association for the Advancement of Science (AAAS) (1990). Science for all Americans. *New York: Oxford University Press.*

American Association for the Advancement of Science (AAAS) (1993). Benchmarks for scientific literacy: Project 2061. *New York: Oxford University Press.*

Biological Sciences Curriculum Study (BSCS) (1970). Biology teacher's handbook. *New York: John Wiley and Sons.*

Bentley, M., Ebert, C., & Ebert, E. (1999). The natural investigator: A constructivist approach to the teaching of elementary and middle school science. *Belmont, California; Wadsworth publishing.*

Black, P & William D. (1998). Inside the Black Box: Raising Standards Through Classroom Assessment.

Black, P & Wiliam, D. (1998). Assessment and Classroom Learning. *Assessment in Education*, March 1998, pp. 7-74.

Bloom, B. (1956). Taxonomy of Educational Objectives, Handbook I: The Cognitive Domain. *New York: David McKay Co Inc.*

Bredderman, T. (1983). Effects of activity-based elementary science on student outcomes: A quantitative analysis. *Review of educational research,* **53(4),** 499-518.

Bresnick, J. (2000). Facilitating inquiry investigations by first graders. *Connect,* **13(4),** 6-8.

Brickhouse, N.W. (1990). Teachers' beliefs about the nature of science and their relationship to classroom practice. *Journal of teacher education,* **41,** 53-62.

Bruner, J.S. (1967). Toward a theory of instruction. *Cambridge, Massachusetts; Harvard University Press.*

Carin, A.A., Bass, J.E., Contant, T.L. (2005). Teaching science as inquiry. *New York; Pearson Education Ltd.*

Chiappetta, E.L. (1997). Inquiry-based science. Strategies and techniques for encouraging inquiry in the classroom. *The science teacher,* **64(10),** 22-26.

Chiappetta, E., Koballa, T., & Collette, A. (1998). Science instruction in the middle and secondary schools. *New York; Merrill publishing group.*

Colburn, A. (1997). How to make lab activities more open ended. *CSTA journal,* Fall 1997, Pages 4-6.

Colburn, A. (2000). An inquiry primer. *Science scope,* March 2000. Pages 42-44.

Costenson, K., Lawson, A.E. (1986). Why isn't inquiry used in more classrooms? *The American biology teacher,* **48(3)**; 150-158.

Chin, C. (2001). Learning in Science: What Do Students' Questions Tell Us About Their Thinking? Education Jounrnal, **29(2),** 85-103.

Cox-Peterson, A.M. & Olson, J.K. (2001). Promoting puzzlement and inquiry with pillbugs. *Science activities,* **37(4),** 20-23.

Crawford, B. A. (1999). Is it realistic to expect a preservice teacher to create an inquiry-based classroom? *Journal of Science Teacher Education,*10,175-194.

Crawford, B. A. (2000). Embracing the Essence of Inquiry: New Roles for Science Teachers. Journal of Research in Science Teaching, 37(9), 916-937.

Cuevas, P., Lee, O., Hart, J., & Deaktor, R. (2003). Improving science inquiry with elementary students of diverse backgrounds. *Journal of research in science teaching*, **42**, 337–357.

Deters, K.M. (2005). Student opinions regarding inquiry-based labs. *Journal of chemical education*, **82(8),** 1178-1180.

Dewey, J. (1933/1998). How we think (Rev. ed.). *Boston, Massachusetts; Houghton Mifflin Company.*

Dillon, J. T. (1988). The remedial status of student questioning. *Journal of Curriculum Studies,* **20(3),** 197-210.

Donaldson, N.L., & Odom, A.L. (2001). What makes swing time? A directed inquiry-based lab assessment. *Science activities,* **38(2),** *29-32.*

Duschl, R.A. (1990). Restructuring science education. *New York; Teachers College Press.*

Eick C.J., & Reed, C.J. (2002). What makes an inquiry-oriented science teacher? The influence of learning histories on student teacher role identity and practise. *Science education*, **86**, 401-416.

Eltinge, E.M., & Roberts, C.W. (1993). Linguistic content analysis: a method to measure science as inquiry in textbooks. *Journal of research in science teaching*, **30(1**), 65-83.

Elstgeest, J. (1985). The right question at the right time. In: *Primary Science; taking the plunge. Oxford, UK; Heinemann Educational Books.*

Favero, T. (1998). Double dipping for research. An introduction to the scientific method. *The American biology teacher*, **60(7),** 524-526.

Fradd, S.H., & Lee, O. (1999). Teachers' roles in promoting science inquiry with students from diverse language backgrounds. *Educational researcher*, **28,** 4–20.

Fradd, S.H., Lee, O., Sutman, F.X., & Saxton, M.K. (2001). Promoting science literacy with English language learners through instructional materials development: A case study. *Billingual Research Journal,* **25 (4),** 417-439.

Gallagher, J.J. (1991). Prospective and practising secondary school science teachers' beliefs about the philosophy of science. *Science education*, **75,** 121-133.

Germann, P.J., Haskins, S., & Auls S. (1996). Analysis of nine high school biology laboratory manuals: promoting scientific inquiry. *Journal of research in science teaching,* **33,** 475- 499.

Gibson, H.L., & Chase, C. (2002). Longitudinal impact of an inquiry-based science program on middle school students' attitudes toward science. *Science education*, **86,** 693–705.

Haury, D.L. (1993). Teaching science through inquiry. ERIC CSMEE Digest (March Ed 359 048).

Harlen, W. (2004). Evaluating inquiry-based science developments. *Paper commissioned by the national research council in preparation for a meeting on the status of evaluation of inquiry-based science education.*

Harlen, W. (2003). Enhancing Inquiry through Formative Assessment. *Paper for the Institute for Inquiry/ Exploratorium, San Francisco, California.*

Harlen, W. (1985). Helping children to plan investigations. In: *Primary science; taking the plunge, edited by Harlen W. Oxford, UK; Heinemann Educational Books.*

Herron, M.D. (1971). The nature of scientific enquiry. *School review,* **79,** 171-212.

Huber, R.A., & Moore, C.J. (2001). A model for extending hands-on science to be inquiry based. *School science and mathematics,* **101(1),** 32-41.

Karplus, R., & Their, H. (1974). SCIS teacher's handbook. *Berkeley, California: Science Curriculum Improvement Study.*

Keys, C.W., & Bryan, L.A. (2001). Co-constructing inquiry-based science with teachers: Essential research for lasting reform. *Journal of research in science teaching,* **38,** 631–645.

Koch, A., & Eckstein, S. G. (1991). Improvement of reading comprehension of physics texts by students' question formulation. *International Journal of Science Education,* **13(4),** 473-486.

Koch, J. (2000). Science stories: Teachers and children as science learners. *Boston, Massachusetts; Houghton Mifflin.*

Krajcik, J., Blumenfeld, P.C., Marx, R.W., Bass, K.M., & Fredricks, J. (1998). Inquiry in project-based science classrooms: Initial attempts by middle school students. *The journal of the learning sciences,* **7 (3&4),** 313-350.

Kyle, W.C.Jr, Bonnstetter, R.,J., & Gadsen, T., Jr (1986). An analysis of elementary students' and teachers' attitudes to ward science in process-approach vs. traditional science classes. *Journal of research in science teaching,* **25,** 103-120.

Lakatos, I. (1970). Falsification and the methodology of scientific research programmes. In I. Lakatos & A. Musgrave (Eds.), Criticism and the growth of knowledge (pp. 91–195). *Cambridge, UK: Cambridge University Press.*

Lawson, A.E. (2000). Managing the inquiry classroom; problems and solutions. *The American biology teacher,* **62(9),** 641-648.

Lederman, N.G., Abd-El-Khalick, F., Bell, R.L., & Schwartz, R.S. (2002). Views of nature of science questionnaire: Toward valid and meaningful assessment of learners' conceptions of nature of science. *Journal of research in science teaching.* **39(6),** 497-521.

Levy, D. (2000). Chemistry teacher captivates young minds with lab theatrics. *Stanford News Service,* **(650),** 725.

Marlow, M.P., Wright, J.L., & Hand, J.D. (2003). A palaeontology network inquiry consortium: Impact on teacher practise. *Journal of geoscience education*, **51(3)**, 317-321.

Marx, R.W., Blumenfeld, P.C., Krajcik, J.S., Fishman, B., Soloway, E., Geier, R., & Tal, R.T. (1998). Inquiry-based science in the middle grades: Assessment of learning in urban systemic reform. *Journal of research in science teaching*. **41**, 1063–1080.

Matyas, M.L. (2000). Teaching and learning by inquiry. *Paper for the American Physiological Society*.

McBride, J.W., Bhatti, M.I., Hannan, M.A., & Feinberg M. (2004). Using an inquiry approach to teach science to secondary school science teachers. *Physics education*, **39(5)**, 434-438.

National Research Council (1996). National science education standards. *Washington, D.C.: National Academy Press*.

National Research Council. (2000). Inquiry and the national science education standards: A guide for teaching and learning. *Washington, D.C.: National Academy Press*.

Osborn, A. (1953). Applied imagination. *New York; Charles Scribner's Sons*.

Palincsar, A.S., Collins, K.M., Marano, N.L., & Magnusson, S.J. (2000). Investigating the engagement and learning of students with learning disabilities in guided inquiry science teaching. *Language, speech, and hearing services in schools*, **31**, 240-251.

Piaget, J. (1969). Science of education and the psychology of the child. *New York: Grossman Publishers*.

Piaget, J. (1954). The construction of reality in the child. *New York: Basic Books*.

Piaget, J. (1959). Judgment and reasoning in the child. *Totowa, New Jersey: Littlefield, Addams & Company*.

Pizzini, E.L. (1991). The inquiry level of junior high activities: implications to science teaching. *Journal of research in science teaching*, **28**, 111-121.

Popper, Karl: (1972). Objective knowledge. *Oxford, UK; Oxford University Press*.

Project 2061. (1993). Benchmarks for science literacy. *New York; Oxford University Press*.

Preddy, L.B. (2006). Student inquiry in the research process. Accessed from http://www.msdpt.k12.in.us/~lpreddy//index.HTM on 25th March 2006.

Rowe, M.B. (1987). Wait-time: Slowing down may be a way of speeding up. *American educator*, **11(1)**, 38-47.

Rutherford, F.J., & Ahlgren, A. (1990). Science for all Americans. *Oxford University Press; New York.*

Sang, D., & Wood-Robinson, V. (2002). Teaching secondary scientific enquiry. *London, UK; ASE/John Murray.*

Sampson, V. (2004). The science management observation protocol. *The science teacher,* March 2004. Pages 30-33.

Scardamalia, M., & Bereiter, C. (1992). Text-based and knowledge-based questioning by children. *Cognition and instruction,* **9 (3)**, 177-199.

Schwab, J.J. (1962). The teaching of science as inquiry, In J.J. Schwab & P.F. Brandweine. The teaching of science. *Cambridge, Massachusetts; Harvard University Press.*

Shymansky, J.A., Kyle, W.C.Jr, & Albert, J.M. (1982). How effective were hands-on science programs of yesterday? *Science and children,* **20(3)**, 13-14.

Shymansky, J. A., Kyle, W.C., & Alport, J.M. (1983). The effects of new science curricula on student performance. *Journal of research in science teaching,* **20**, 387-404.

Shymansky, J.A., Hedges, L.V., & Woodworth, G. (1990). A reassessment of the effects of inquiry-based science curricula of the '60s on student performance. *Journal of research in science teaching,* **27**, 127-144.

Sutman, F.X., Schmuckler, J.S., Hilosky, A., Priestley, W.J., Priestley, H., & White M. (1998). Evaluating the use of the inquiry matrix. *Paper presented at the Annual Conference of the National Association for Research in Science Teaching, San Diego, California.*

Smith, M.U., & Scharmann, L.C. (1999). Defining versus describing the nature of science: A pragmatic analysis for classroom teachers and science educators. *Science education,* **83**, 493–509.

Tafoya E., Sunal, D., & Knecht, P. (1980). Assessing inquiry potential: a tool for curriculum decision makers. *School science and mathematics,* **80**, 43-48.

TERC (1998). Light energy for life: On earth and other worlds? *Hands on!* Volume **23(1).**

Thomas K., Davis C., & Thomas J. (2005). Plant and animal interrelationships. UCLA, GK-12 Science and mathematics in Los Angeles urban schools. *Accessed 15.12.2005 from http://www.nslc.ucla.edu/STEP/GK12/.*

Tobin, K., & McRobbie, C.J. (1996). Cultural myths as constraints to the enacted science curriculum. *Science education,* **80**, 223-241.

Volkmann, M.J., & Abell, S.K. (2003). Rethinking laboratories. Tools for converting cookbook labs into inquiry. *The science teacher,* September 2003, 38-40.

Von Secker, C.E., & Lissitz, R.W. (1999). Estimating the impact of instructional practices on student achievement in science. *Journal of research in science teaching*, **36**, 1110-1126.

Von Secker, C. (2002). Effects of inquiry-based teaching practises on science excellence and equity. *Journal of educational research*, **95**, 151-160.

Vygotsky, L. S. (1962). Thought and language. *Cambridge, Massachusetts: The MIT Press.*

Welch, W., Klopfer, L., Aikenhead G., & Robinson, I. (1981). The role of inquiry in science education: analysis and recommendations. *Science education*, **65**, 33-50.

Wolfinger, D. (1999). Science in the elementary and middle school. *New York; Pearson Education Publishing.*

Windschitl, M. (2003). Inquiry projects in science teacher education: What can investigative experiences reveal about teacher thinking and eventual classroom practice? *Science education*, **87(1)**, 112-143.